LAKES AND WETLANDS

THE LIVING EARTH

LAKES AND WETLANDS

EDITED BY JOHN P. RAFFERTY, ASSOCIATE EDITOR, EARTH AND LIFE SCIENCES

Britannica®
Educational Publishing

IN ASSOCIATION WITH

ROSEN
EDUCATIONAL SERVICES

Published in 2011 by Britannica Educational Publishing
(a trademark of Encyclopædia Britannica, Inc.)
in association with Rosen Educational Services, LLC
29 East 21st Street, New York, NY 10010.

First Edition

Britannica Educational Publishing
Michael I. Levy: Executive Editor
J.E. Luebering: Senior Manager
Marilyn L. Barton: Senior Coordinator, Production Control
Steven Bosco: Director, Editorial Technologies
Lisa S. Braucher: Senior Producer and Data Editor
Yvette Charboneau: Senior Copy Editor
Kathy Nakamura: Manager, Media Acquisition
John P. Rafferty: Associate Editor, Earth Sciences

Rosen Educational Services
Jeanne Nagle: Senior Editor
Nelson Sá: Art Director
Cindy Reiman: Photography Manager
Matthew Cauli: Designer, Cover Design
Introduction by David Nagle

Library of Congress Cataloging-in-Publication Data

Lakes and wetlands / edited by John P. Rafferty.—1st ed.
    p. cm.—(The living earth)
"In association with Britannica Educational Publishing, Rosen Educational Services."
Includes bibliographical references and index.
ISBN 978-1-61530-320-5 (library binding)
1. Lakes 2. Lake ecology. 3. Wetlands. 4. Wetland ecology. I. Rafferty, John P.
GB1603.7.L35 2011
551.48'2—dc22

2010023017

Manufactured in the United States of America

Cover Shutterstock.com

On pages x: *Everglades Natural Park in Florida, U.S. National Park Service*

On pages v, 1, 42, 64, 80, 132, 153, 179, 212, 213, 214, 223: A freshwater marsh, dominated
by saw grass and dotted by palms and cypresses, in the Everglades, southern Florida, U.S.
Jeff Greenberg/Peter Arnold, Inc.

CONTENTS

Introduction   x

Chapter 1: Lakes   1
Limnology: The Study of Fresh
Waters   3
     The History of Lakes   4
     The Physical Characteristics of
     Lakes   4
     Water and Energy Fluxes
     in Lakes   6
     The Water Quality of Lakes   7
Lake Basins   7
     The Classification of Basins   7
     Evaporites   8
     Basin Topography   18
     Sediments and Sedimentation   19
Lake Waters   23
     Chemical Composition   23
     Thermal Properties   28
     Eutrophication   29
     Vertical Mixing and Overturn   30
     The Heat Budget of Lakes   32
     Heat Transfer   35
Uses and Abuses of Lakes   37
     Economy and Ecology   38
     Problems and Effects   40

Chapter 2: Lake Hydraulics   42
Currents   42
     Pressure Gradients   43
     Wind Stress   44
     Internal Waves and Langmuir
     Circulation   45

3

15

39

Surface Waves   46
Seiches   48
The Effects of Wave and Current
Action   50
The Hydrologic Balance of
the Lakes   52
    The Water Budget   53
    Water-Level Fluctuations 59
    Lake Extinction   62

**Chapter 3: Inland Water
Ecosystems**   64
The Origin of Inland Waters   64
Permanent Bodies of Standing
Fresh Water   66
Temporary Bodies of Standing
Fresh Water   70
Saline Lakes   71
The Biota of Inland Waters   73
The Structure of Inland Water
Ecosystems   75
The Biological Productivity of
Inland Water Ecosystems   77

**Chapter 4: Major Lakes of
the World**   80
Dead Sea   80
Caspian Sea   86
    Physical Features   87
    Study and Exploration   94
Great Bear Lake   95
The Great Lakes   96
    Lake Erie   97
    Lake Huron   99
    Lake Michigan   101
    Lake Ontario   103

Lake Superior 105
Lake Agassiz 109
Great Salt Lake 109
Great Slave Lake 112
Lake Baikal 113
Lake Balkhash 116
Lake Chad 119
    Geology and Physiography 120
    Climate 120
    Hydrology 121
    Plant Life 123
    Animal Life 123
    Study and Exploration 125
Lake Nyasa 126
Lake Tanganyika 127
Lake Victoria 129
Lake Winnipeg 131

Chapter 5: Wetlands 132
Coastal Systems 132
    Mangrove Swamps 133
    Salt Marshes 134
    The Rann of Kachchh 137
    Freshwater Tidal Marshes 137
    Seaweed-Based Systems 138
    Sea-Grass Beds 142
    Beaches and Mudflats 143
Inland Wetland Systems 144
    Freshwater Marshes 145
    Pantanal 146
    Bogs and Fens 146
    Peat and Peat Moss 147
    Forested Swamps 149
    Riparian Systems 149
Wetland Management 150
Wetland Ecology 151

Chapter 6: Wetland Flora and Fauna   153

  Bog Biota   153
    Heaths   154
  Marsh Flora   155
  Animals of the Marsh   157
  Trees and Other Plants of the Swamp   157
  Salt Swamp Flora   158
  Swamp Fauna   162
  Specific Wetland Regions   162
    Bangweulu   163
    Big Cypress Swamp   163
    Congaree National Park   164
    The Everglades   165
    Great Dismal Swamp   167
    Himmerland   169
    Lake Ḥammār   170
    Okavango Delta   171
    Okefenokee Swamp   172
    Pripet Marshes   173
    Sundarbans   175
    Zoigê Marsh   175
  Conclusion   176

Appendix A: Notable Smaller Lakes of the World   179

  Hongze Lake   179
  Koko Nor   180
  Lake Como   183
  Lake Constance   184
  Lake Edward   185
  Lake Eyre   186
  Lake Garda   187
  Lake Geneva   188
  Lake Ladoga   189
  Lake Maggiore   191

Lake Maracaibo   192
Lake Managua   193
Lake Nasser   194
Lake Nicaragua   194
Lake Onega   197
Lake Rudolf   199
Lake Tai   200
Lake Titicaca   201
Lake Urmia   204
Lake Van   205
Lake Winnipegosis   207
Lake Ysyk   208
Tonle Sap   210

**Appendix B: Average Net
Primary Production of the
Earth's Major Habitats**

212

**Appendix C: Areas and Volumes
of the Great Lakes**

213

Glossary   214
Bibliography   216
Index   223

INTRODUCTION

Life on Earth is dependent upon many things, not the least of which is water. It follows, then, that the study of the fresh waters of Earth, called limnology, is important to understanding the ways in which water affects humans and their physical surroundings. As the pages of this book bear out, lakes are complex, ever-changing phenomena worthy of considerable and intricate study. This volume also examines the regions where water meets dry land, forming wetlands, both fresh and saline.

Lakes are born when water fills a depression formed by natural means or human activity. Lake basins result from volcanic activity; shifting land masses; the movement of glaciers; erosion by wind, water, or animals; human activity such as mining; or even by being blasted into existence by a flaming meteorite. Lakes undergo continual change to their chemical makeup and physical structure, sometimes at a rate that is unnoticeable but actual nonetheless. They start out as simple holding pens for water with almost no life (oligotrophic stage). After accumulating nutrients from dust in the air or sediment from streams, biological activity increases, which results in poorer water quality (eutrophic stage). Over time, lakes are filled in with sediment that washes in from upstream sources and organic material. Eventually, they disappear, often becoming wet meadows and forests. Human activity can accelerate this naturally slow process through the introduction of nutrients and fertilizers.

Not surprisingly, lake water is made up of many different substances in addition to the base water. While all lakes have water in common, it is the varying concentrations of other substances that set one lake apart from another. The salt concentration, or salinity, of the water is one such variable. Salinity refers to the concentration of ions—charged atoms or molecules—present in water. Certain lakes, such as Great Salt Lake in Utah (U.S.) and the Dead Sea in the Middle East, have salinity levels higher than that of the world's oceans. The majority of lakes, however, have ion concentrations so low that salinity level becomes negligible. Soluble salts in the surrounding rock, which gradually erodes and flows into lakes via streams and rivers, determine salinity. Many other inorganic compounds such as various plant nutrients (e.g., phosphates and nitrates), heavy metals (e.g., mercury), and polychlorinated hydrocarbons (e.g., DDT) may also find their way into a lake by these means, although rainfall and wind-borne air particulates are culprit methods of addition as well.

Numerous interacting variables influence the life cycle of a lake, among them temperature variants within lake strata and the extent to which light penetrates into the deeper waters. Solar radiation, inflows and outflows of water, and the effects of wind cause temperature change; currents and wave action each directly affects the temperature map of a lake. These temperature zones within lakes are further affected by clastic sediments (clay, silt, sand), organic debris, and chemical precipitates. In general, lakes undergo heat transfers vertically, which causes mixing of the waters to the extent that thermocline, or heat-gradient, regions will "flip." For example, the uppermost lake waters, characterized by temperatures near freezing (0 °C [32 °F]) in the early spring, absorb heat as the weather warms. The density of the water in these upper layers will increase until the water temperature exceeds (4 °C [39.2 °F]). If the density of the upper layers of the lake is greater than that of the lower layers, the water in the upper layers sinks, and the lake water overturns.

While heat transfer mechanisms can be observed and quantified, the influence of surface heat and moisture, water pressure, and atmospheric stability among other variables remains poorly understood. One might say that it is difficult to be exact in such a "fluid" environment. As a liquid, water is in constant motion. Lake water responds to various outside physical forces by displacing vertically, horizontally, or both. Water movement is primarily caused by wind action at the surface, and differences in heating between one region of the lake and the next, Earth's rotation, water inflow and outflow—just about anything and everything that interacts with lake water—can also cause it to move. These phenomena result in surface waves, internal waves, currents, or seiching, which is the tendency of a body of water to refill an area left devoid of water as a result of the water movement. These processes are responsible for the reshaping of lakes by erosion and sediment deposition, which creates deltas, sand bars, and spits.

Lakes continue to exist due to the hydrological balance between water additions and losses. This "water budget" must always be taken into consideration when changes such as dredging and damming occur within a lake basin. While natural, ongoing changes to a lake's water budget—evaporation, precipitation, groundwater flow rates—are, for the most part, uncontrollable and must be considered before any engineering project begins.

Water generally enters a lake via streams, rivers, precipitation, and groundwater. The importance of each source can vary greatly from lake to lake. Water exits a lake either through surface or groundwater flows and evaporation. If a lake is considered "closed," that is, without groundwater or surface outlets, only the latter process is ongoing. Lakes in which evaporation and outlets occur are deemed "open." The extent to which the water level of any particular lake will fluctuate is dependent upon many factors, but seasonality, in general, is a key factor in water levels. During regular periods of precipitation, water levels will rise and will lower during times of little precipitation.

As mentioned, lakes metamorph from oligotrophic states to eutrophic states over the course of a life cycle that can last for eons. Many factors have a role in this process, which is measured by oxygen level. The oxygen content of a lake often determines the lake's position along the oligotrophic-eutrophic continuum. As organic material increases, there is a greater demand on lake oxygen to sustain aqautic life, and bottom sediments become increasingly enriched in organic material. Over time, sediments and organic materials accumulate and thus make portions of the lake shallower. Aquatic plants that root themselves to the bottom of the lake take advantage of these shallow areas and infill lakeward. The resulting marsh continues to expand as more organic material and sediment fills in the deeper areas of the lake. The lake first declines into a pond and then shrinks away completely. Such is the way of most all lakes on Earth.

Wetlands, which are areas "betwixt and between" water and land, are difficult to define because of their changing physical states. Characterized by shallow water, saturated soil, vegetation that has adapted to wet conditions, and soil that slows or stops organic decomposition, wetlands can at times appear as dry meadows or shrub areas that have been intermittently flooded. The United States government has determined that to be called a wetland an area must be "inundated or saturated with a frequency and duration sufficient to support a prevalence of vegetation typically adapted for life in saturated conditions." There must also be standing water or saturated soils for at least part of the growing season. Wetlands comprise about 4 percent to 6 percent of Earth's land surface, and can be categorized as either coastal or inland, depending upon location. Coastal wetlands may be subcategorized as mangroves, freshwater tidal marshes, and salt marshes.Mangrove swamps are found in warmer latitudes and are so called due to colonization by mangrove trees, which have aboveground root systems that make for an impenetrable wall for larger creatures. The decaying mangrove leaves, algae, seaweed, and mud that form the substrate upon which these trees grow provide a wonderful habitat for smaller oceanic fauna. Crabs, shrimp, clams, and snails abound in these areas.

In contrast, freshwater tidal marshes are similar to salt marshes but far enough removed from the coastline that salt stress is much lower. Such areas include rivers which are affected by oceanic tides. With higher plant diversity and rich animal life, these areas provide freshwater and sea access—the same traits that many people are likely to find attractive. These areas, not surprisingly, are considered to be the most altered by urban development. As a result, wetlands are increasingly the places marked for restoration and protection. A closer look at one of the largest and historically most productive freshwater marsh areas in the United States, Chesapeake Bay, serves as an example of a wetland system facing the problem of urban development.

Salt marshes diverge from mangrove marshes in that they are dominated by taller grasses rooted in the alternately drying and submerging soil areas. Found in higher latitudes than mangroves, these areas are some of the richest ecosystems in the world, characterized by tremendous plankton, fish, and invertebrate diversity. They are rich in nutrients, which are exchanged through various channels between dry land and marine habitats. Various other important boundary ecosystems that are not themselves wetlands, such as seagrass beds, coastal mudflats, and seaweed-based ecosystems, interact with salt marshes along coasts.

The eponymous vegetation in seaweed-based areas vary in size from those that are almost microscopic to giant kelp over 130 feet long. Defending shorelines—and, thus, the salt marshes they border—by their absorption of wave action, kelp form beds in which a rich diversity of animal life reside. Sea-grass beds exist just below low-tide mark in all latitudes. As tides recede or approach, these grasses slow incoming water, which allows larger amounts of sediment and silt to settle. This material provides habitat for clams and worms. When the sea grass dies, they are decomposed by a fungal and bacterial "soup," thereby recycling nutrients. Sea-grass beds supply homes for threatened species, such as manatees, dugongs, and green sea turtles. Beaches and mudflats behind the sea-grass beds consist of sediments that are simply too unstable to support much plant life. This lack of floral diversity, however, is not reflected in the importance or diversity of a particular mudflat's fauna. At high tide, various sea predators use the flats as hunting grounds, seeking out the clams, worms, and burrowing shrimp that inhabit them. It is these creatures—the burrowers, as well as some tardy predators—that many migratory and local birds use as a food source.

Inland wetland systems consist of freshwater marshes, bogs, fens, forested swamps, and riparian plant communities. Bogs consist of peat, a form of partially decayed plant matter. Having a high water table and no significant inflow or outflow, these areas are characterized by water with a low pH. Thus, bogs are acidic environments. Located throughout the Northern Hemisphere, bogs usually have a false surface consisting of a mat of vegetation, under which lies clear water. Fens, in contrast, are essentially bogs that receive drainage from surrounding mineral soils and, as a result, are more likely than not to be covered by grasses, reeds, or sedges.

Forested swamps are, as the name implies, dominated by trees and other woody vegetation that can tolerate flooding on a regular basis. Cypress trees, swamp tupelo, and, to an extent, maple trees are examples of such flora. Riparian systems, which are also called riverine systems, are located along rivers that regularly flood their surrounding areas. They can be wide alluvial valleys or small vegetative strips closely following the source stream or river. As one might imagine, these areas are particularly valuable to wildlife as sources of water, food, and cover, especially during periods of migration.

Lakes and wetlands have been used by humans for millennia. Throughout the world, these valuable areas have served as sources of drinking water, food, fuel (peat), and construction materials. Wetlands resources have been used to run farms, culture fish, and, in many cases, protect areas further inland. They are among the world's most productive ecosystems, and among the most economically valuable ecosystems for humans. Any threat to the world's wetlands — such as that posed by the Deepwater Horizon drilling rig explosion in 2010 and the subsequent release of massive amounts of oil into the Gulf of Mexico — can adversely affect large segments of human populations as well as the diverse group of plants and animals that reside within them. Thus, wetlands management is increasingly seen as a valuable conservation activity. Many experts argue that wetlands management should not be left to narrow interest groups, but open to numerous sources of input. That is, arguably, the best way to determine the best courses of action in order to support and maintain these incredibly complex ecosystems.

CHAPTER 1
LAKES

A lake is a relatively large body of slowly moving or standing water that occupies an inland basin of appreciable size. Definitions that precisely distinguish lakes, ponds, swamps, and even rivers and other bodies of non-oceanic water are not well established. It may be said, however, that rivers and streams are relatively fast moving; marshes and swamps contain relatively large quantities of grasses, trees, or shrubs; and ponds are relatively small in comparison to lakes. Geologically defined, lakes are temporary bodies of water.

Within the global hydrologic cycle, freshwater lakes play a very small quantitative role, constituting only about 0.009 percent of all free water, which amounts to less than 0.4 percent of all continental fresh water. Saline lakes and inland seas contain another 0.0075 percent of all free water. Freshwater lakes, however, contain well over 98 percent of the important surface waters available for use. Apart from that contained in saline bodies, most other continental waters are tied up in glaciers and ice sheets and the remainder is in groundwater.

Four-fifths of the 125,000 cubic km (30,000 cubic miles) of lake waters occur in a small number of lakes, perhaps 40 in all. Among the largest are Lake Baikal, in Central Asia, containing about 23,000 cubic km (5,500 cubic miles) of water; Lake Tanganyika (19,000 cubic km [4,600 cubic miles]), in eastern Africa; and Lake Superior (12,000 cubic km [2,900 cubic miles]), one of the Great Lakes of North America. The Great Lakes contain a total of about 25,000 cubic km (6,000 cubic miles) of water and, together with other North American lakes larger than 10 cubic km (2 cubic miles), constitute about one-fourth of the world's lake waters. The Caspian Sea, though not considered a lake by some hydrologists, is the world's largest inland sea. Located in Central Asia, the Caspian Sea has an area of about 386,000 square km (149,000 square miles).

Although lakes are to be found throughout the world, the continents of North America, Africa, and Asia contain about 70 percent of the total lake water, the other continents being less generously endowed. A fourth of the total volume of lake water is spread throughout the world in uncounted numbers of small lakes. Anyone who has flown over much of the Canadian plains area cannot help but be struck by the seemingly endless skein of lakes and ponds covering the landscape below. Though the total volume of water involved is comparatively small, the surface area of lake water is substantial. The total surface area of all Canadian lakes has been estimated to exceed the total surface area of the province of Alberta. The U.S. state of Alaska has more than 3 million lakes with surface areas greater than 8 hectares (20 acres).

The larger, deeper lakes are a significant factor within the cycle of water—from rain to surface water, ice, soil moisture, or groundwater and thence to water vapour. These lakes receive the drainage from vast tracts of land, store it, pass it on seaward, or lose it to the atmosphere by evaporation. On a local basis, even the smaller lakes play an important hydrologic role. The relatively high ratio of exposed surface area to the total water volume of these lakes accentuates their effectiveness as evaporators.

In some cases the efficiency of lakes in losing water to the atmosphere is locally undesirable, because of public and industrial requirements for lake water. A striking example of this condition is the Aral Sea, located in Central Asia. Although it is still one of the world's largest bodies of inland water, in the second half of the 20th century its area was reduced by two-fifths and its mean surface

Africa's Lake Chad, the largest lake in Africa. Chad's water levels fluctuate with the seasons, since they are dependent upon the vagaries of the hydrologic cycle within a typically arid climate. © Kypros/Alamy

level had dropped by more than 12 metres (40 feet), as a result primarily of the diversion of the Syr Darya and Amu Darya rivers for irrigating adjoining fields.

In some basins (e.g., the Chad basin in Africa), lakes are the terrestrial end point of the hydrologic cycle. With no outflow downstream toward the oceans, these closed lakes swell or recede according to the balance of local hydrologic conditions.

LIMNOLOGY: THE STUDY OF FRESH WATERS

Limnology is a subdiscipline of hydrology that deals with the scientific study of fresh waters, specifically those found in lakes and ponds. The discipline also includes the biological, physical, and chemical aspects of the occurrence of lake and pond waters. Limnology traditionally is closely related to hydrobiology, which is concerned with the application of the principles and methods of physics, chemistry, geology, and geography to ecological problems.

THE HISTORY OF LAKES

A newly formed lake generally contains few nutrients and can sustain only a small amount of biomass. It is described as oligotrophic. Natural processes will supply nutrients to a lake in solution in river water and rainwater, in the fallout of dust from the atmosphere, and in association with the sediments washed into the lake. The lake will gradually become eutrophic, with relatively poor water quality and high biological production. Infilling by sediments means that the lake will gradually become shallower and eventually disappear. Natural rates of eutrophication are normally relatively slow. Human activities, however, can greatly accelerate the process by the addition of excessive nutrients in wastewater and the residues of agricultural fertilizers. The result may be excessive biomass production, as evidenced by phytoplankton "blooms" and rapid growth of macrophytes such as *Eichhornia*.

THE PHYSICAL CHARACTERISTICS OF LAKES

The most important physical characteristic of the majority of lakes is their pattern of temperatures, in particular, the changes of temperature with depth. The vertical profile of temperature may be measured using arrays of temperature probes deployed either from a boat or from a stationary platform. Remote-sensing techniques are being used increasingly to observe patterns of temperature in space and, in particular, to identify the thermal plumes associated with thermal pollution.

In summer the water of many lakes becomes stratified into a warmer upper layer, called the epilimnion, and a cooler lower layer, called the hypolimnion. The stratification plays a major role in the movement of nutrients and dissolved oxygen and has an important control effect on lake ecology. Between the layers there usually exists a zone of very rapid temperature change known as the thermocline. When the lake begins to cool at the end of summer, the cooler surface water tends to sink because it has greater density. Eventually this results in an overturn of the stratification and a mixing of the layers. Temperature change with depth is generally much smaller in winter. Some lakes, called dimictic lakes, can also exhibit a spring overturn following the melting of ice cover, since water has a maximum density at 4 °C (39 °F).

A second important characteristic of lakes is the way that the availability of light changes with depth. Light decreases exponentially (as described by Beer's law) depending on the turbidity of the water. At the compensation depth the light available for photosynthetic production is just matched by the energy lost in respiration. Above this depth is the euphotic zone, but below it in the aphotic zone phytoplankton—the lowest level in the ecological system of a lake—cannot survive unless the organisms are capable of vertical migration.

Patterns of sediment deposition in lakes depend on the rates of supply in inflowing waters and on subsurface currents and topography. Repetitive sounding of the lake bed may be used to investigate patterns of sedimentation. Remote sensing of the turbidity of the surface waters also has been used to infer rates of sedimentation, as in the artificial Lake Nasser in Egypt. In some parts of the world where erosion rates are high, the operational life of reservoirs may be reduced dramatically by infilling with sediment.

WATER AND ENERGY FLUXES IN LAKES

The water balance of a lake may be evaluated by considering an extended form of the catchment water balance equation outlined above with additional terms for any natural or artificial inflows. An energy balance equation may be defined in a similar way, including terms for the exchange of long-wave and shortwave radiation with the Sun and atmosphere and for the transport of sensible and latent heat associated with convection and evaporation. Heat also is gained and lost with any inflows and discharges from the lake. The energy balance equation controls the thermal regime of the lake and consequently has an important effect on the ecology of the lake.

An important role in controlling the distribution of temperature in a lake is played by currents due either to the action of the wind blowing across the surface of the lake or to the effect of the inflows and outflows, especially where, for example, a lake receives the cooling water from a power-generation plant. In large lakes the effect of the Earth's rotation has an important effect on the flow of water within the lake. The action of the wind can also result in the formation of waves and, when surface water is blown toward a shore, in an accumulation of water that causes a rise in water level called wind setup. In Lake Erie in North America, increases in water level of more than one metre (3.3 feet) have been observed following severe storms. After a storm the water raised in this way causes a seiche (an oscillatory wave of long period) to travel across the lake and back. Seiches are distinctive features of such long, narrow lakes as Lake Zürich, when the wind blows along the axis of the lake. Internal seiche waves can occur in stratified lakes with layers of different density.

THE WATER QUALITY OF LAKES

The biological health of a lake is crucially dependent on its chemical characteristics. Limnologists and hydrobiologists are attentive to the dissolved oxygen content of the water because it is a primary indicator of water quality. Well-oxygenated water is considered to be of good quality. Low dissolved oxygen content results in anaerobic fermentation, which releases such gases as toxic hydrogen sulfide into the water, with a drastic effect on biological processes.

Another major concern of limnologists and hydrobiologists is the cycling of basic nutrients within a lake system, particularly carbon, nitrogen, phosphorus, and sulfate. An excess of the latter in runoff waters entering a lake may result in high concentrations of hydrogen ions in the water. Such acid (low values of pH) waters are harmful to the lake biology. In particular, aluminium compounds are soluble in water at low pH and may cause fish to die because of the response induced in their gills.

LAKE BASINS

In addition to the water in lakes and ponds, limnologists also concern themselves with the study of the basins in which the water is held. Lake basins are classified by the forces and processes involved in their creation. The topography and the processes that drive sedimentation in lake basins are also important topics of study since they affect the behaviour of lake waters and provide significant insight into how lakes evolve over time.

THE CLASSIFICATION OF BASINS

Limnologists have used several criteria for the development of systems for classifying lakes and lake basins but have

EVAPORITES

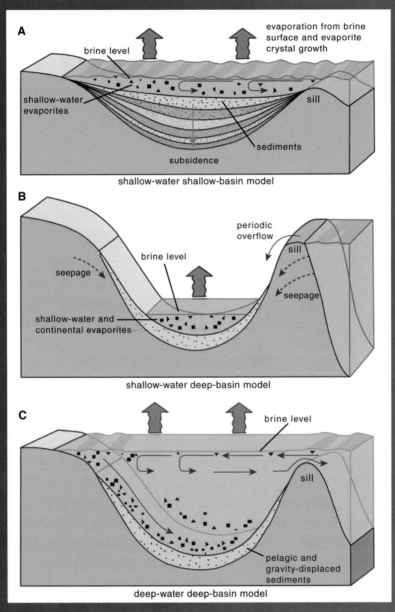

Three models for deposition of marine evaporites in basins of restricted water circulation. Copyright Encyclopædia Britannica; rendering for this edition by Rosen Educational Services.

Evaporites are any of a variety of individual minerals found in the sedimentary deposit of soluble salts that results from the evaporation of water.

Typically, evaporite deposits occur in closed marine basins where evaporation exceeds inflow. The deposits often show a repeated sequence of minerals, indicating cyclic conditions with a mineralogy determined by solubility. The most important minerals and the sequence in which they form include calcite, gypsum, anhydrite, halite, polyhalite, and lastly potassium and magnesium salts such as sylvite, carnallite, kainite, and kieserite; anhydrite and halite dominate. These sequences have been reproduced in laboratory experiments and, therefore, the physical and chemical conditions for evaporite formation are well known.

In contrast to basin deposits, extensive thin-shelf deposits are known and are thought to be the result of shallow, ephemeral seas. Non-marine evaporites formed by streams flowing into closed depressions, especially in arid regions, give rise to deposits of borates, nitrates, and sodium carbonates. Such deposits occur in Utah and southern California in the United States.

resorted particularly to the mechanisms that have produced lake basins. These have been summarized and examined in *A Treatise on Limnology*, by the American limnologist G.E. Hutchinson, which includes treatment of tectonism, volcanism, landslides, glaciation, solution, river action, wind action, coastline building, organic accumulation, animal activity, meteoritic impact, and human activity.

BASINS FORMED BY TECTONISM, VOLCANISM, AND LANDSLIDES

Tectonism—or movement of the Earth's crust—has been responsible for the formation of very large basins. Late in the Miocene Epoch (about 23 to 5.3 million years ago), broad, gentle earth movements resulted in the isolation of a vast inland sea across southern Asia and southeastern Europe. Through the Paleogene and Neogene periods (from about 65.5 million to 2.6 million years ago), sub-basins developed that gradually were characterized by a great range of salinities. Resumption of communication with the oceans occurred later, and there is evidence of considerable variation in water levels. The present remnants of these inland bodies of water include the Caspian Sea and the Aral Sea, along with numerous smaller lakes. The Black Sea, which was also once part of this large inland basin, is now in direct communication with the oceans.

In some cases, elevated land areas may already contain depressions that eventually form lake basins. Lake Okeechobee, Florida, is cited as being such a basin, formed by uplift of the ocean floor.

Tectonic uplift may interfere with natural land-drainage patterns in such a way as to produce lake basins. The Great Basin of South Australia, some of the lakes in Central Africa (e.g., Lakes Kioga and Kwania), and to some extent Lake Champlain, in the northeastern United States, are examples of this mechanism. Land subsidence, due to earthquake activity, also has resulted in the development of depressions in which lakes have evolved. Many such cases have been reported within the past 300 years.

The damming of valleys as a result of various tectonic phenomena has resulted in the formation of a few lake basins, but faulting, in its great variety of forms, has been responsible for the formation of many important lake basins. Abert Lake, in Oregon, lies in the depression formed by a tilted fault block against the higher block. Indeed, many lakes in the western United States are located in depressions formed through faulting, including Lake Tahoe, in the Sierra Nevada, California. Great Salt Lake, Utah, and other nearby salt lakes are remnants of Lake Bonneville, a large lake of Pleistocene age (i.e., about

11,700 to 2,600,000 years old) which was formed at least partly by faulting activity.

In other parts of the world, faulting has also played an important role in basin formation. Lake Baikal and Lake Tanganyika, the two deepest lakes in the world, occupy basins formed by complexes of grabens (downdropped faulted blocks). These lakes are among the oldest of modern lakes, as are other graben lakes, particularly those within the East African rift system, which extends through the East African lake system and includes the Red Sea.

Basins formed from volcanic activity are also greatly varied in type. The emanation of volcanic material from beneath the surface can be explosive, or it can issue in a gentle and regular manner. This range of activity and the variation of types of material which may be involved produce many different types of basins.

Momotombo Volcano (left) and Momotombito Island, viewed across Lake Managua, Nicaragua. Byron Augustin/D. Donne Bryant Stock

One broad category includes those occupying the actual volcanic craters or their remnants. Crater lakes may occupy completely unmodified cinder cones, but these are rare. Craters caused by explosions or by the collapse of the roofs of underground magma (molten silica) chambers and those caused by explosion of new volcanic sources and that are built of nonvolcanic material are other examples. The latter are termed maars, following the local name for such forms in Germany. They are found, however, in several locations, including Iceland, Italy, and New Zealand. The maars of the volcanic district of Eifel, Western Germany, are among the best known of these formations.

The collapse of magma chambers and the development of very large surface craters called calderas is an important source of lake basins. Crater Lake, Oregon, is a typical example, exhibiting characteristically great depth and a high encircling rim. Some caldera basins evolved with gently sloping sides, however, due to the deposition of material from a series of explosions and a gentler collapse of the structure. Secondary cones may develop within calderas, as shown by Wizard Island, in Crater Lake. The largest caldera in the world, which contains Lake Toba, in Sumatra, was formed through a combination of volcanic action and tectonic activity. Lake Toba's basin is contained in a strike-slip fault belt along the entire length of the Barisan Mountains of Sumatra. A vast, initial eruption of lava under gas pressure collapsed the magma reservoir, forming a depression that filled with water, producing the lake. Renewed volcanic activity subsequently led to the formation of an island in the centre, but a second collapse later cut it in two. Additional tectonic activity has further modified the lake's configuration.

Lake basins may also arise from the action of lava flows that emanate from volcanic fissures or craters. Lake Mývatyn, in Iceland, was formed in a basin arising from the collapse of the interior part of a large lava flow. Other basins have formed as the result of volcanic damming. This usually happens where a lava flow interrupts the existing drainage pattern.

Lake basins also may form following the blockage of a drainage depression by landslides. These may be temporary in nature because of the eroding action of the lake on the damming material. Lake Sārez in the Pamirs is stable, being dammed by a rockslide.

BASINS FORMED BY GLACIATION

The basin-forming mechanism responsible for the most abundant production of lakes, particularly in the Northern Hemisphere, is glaciation. The Pleistocene glaciers, which seem to have affected every continent, were especially effective in North America, Europe, and Asia. The retreat of ice sheets produced basins through mechanical action and through the damming effect of their ice masses at their boundaries.

In some cases, lakes actually exist in basins made of ice. In other cases, water masses may form within ice masses. Such occurrences are rare and are not very stable. Damming by ice masses is a more common phenomenon but is also likely to be relatively temporary. Glacial moraine (heterogeneous sedimentary deposits at glacier margins) is also responsible for the occurrence of dammed lake basins. The Finger Lakes of New York State are dammed by an endmoraine.

Ice sheets moving over relatively level surfaces have produced large numbers of small lake basins through scouring in many areas. This type of glacial rock basin contains what are known as ice-scour lakes and is represented in North America by basins in parts of the high Sierras and in west central Canada (e.g., near Great Slave Lake). Tens of thousands of these lakes are found in the ice-scoured regions of the world. Many of them are inter-connected with short streams and may contain narrow inlets. Characteristically, they may be dotted with numer-ous islands and sprawling bays. Many are comparatively shallow. Where they are particularly abundant, they may cover up to 75 percent of the total surface, as in Quetico canoe country of Minnesota.

Glacier scouring associated with the freezing and thawing of névé (granular snow adjacent to glacier ice) at the head of a glaciated valley may produce a deepened cir-cular basin termed a cirque. These are found in widely scattered mountain locations. The action of glaciers in valleys can produce a similar type of basin, often occurring in series and resembling a valley staircase. Ice movement from valleys through narrow openings has produced another type of rock basin, known as glint lake basins, particularly in Scandinavian regions.

Piedmont and fjord (i.e., a river valley that has been "drowned" by a rise of sea level) lakes are found in basins formed by glacial action in long mountain valleys. Excellent examples are found in Norway, the English Lake District, the European Alps, and the Andes. In North America, several regions contain this type of lake basin. In British Columbia, many good examples exist, the largest of which are the Okanagan and Kootenay systems. These are long, narrow lakes of substantial depth. In northwestern Canada, some of the largest lakes, including Lake Athabaska, Great Slave Lake, and Great Bear Lake, are of this type, although they are not found in the same type of mountainous terrain. These lakes, as well as the North American Great Lakes, resulted from the movements of large ice sheets that deepened existing valleys.

The Wisconsin (latest stage of Pleistocene glaciation) ice sheet was responsible for shaping the present Great Lakes system, which drains mainly eastward to the Atlantic

Hornsund Fjord in Svalbard, Norway. The slow movement of glaciers scraped out fjord basins, which were then flooded as sea levels rose. Ralph Lee Hopkins/National Geographic Image Collection

through the St. Lawrence River, during its retreat. The principal stages in the history of these lakes have received much study, and several stages of retreat and advance of the ice sheet have been identified. Behind the lobes of the ice sheet, ice lakes developed that drained according to the modifications of preexisting valleys for glacial action. As the mass of ice retreated far to the north, glacial rebound (uplift of the Earth's crust in response to removal of the loading by ice) caused a general tilting of the land surface. The new lake basins also contributed to the subsequent changes through their own erosional action.

The material comprising glacial moraines or glacial outwash may provide dams that confine postglacial waters. The Finger Lakes, in New York State, constitute one interesting group of this type. These lakes were formed through glacial scouring of existing valleys, which were blocked at both the northern and southern ends by morainic deposits.

A variety of basin types have been formed in the different types of glacial drift deposits, including basins in morainic material, kettle lakes, channels formed by water movement in tunnels beneath the ice masses, and lake basins formed by thawing in permafrost. An interesting example of glacial action is the formation of giant's kettles; these are glacial potholes in the form of deep cylindrical holes. Their origin is still uncertain. Sand, gravel, or boulders are sometimes found at their bottom. The kettles vary from a few centimetres to a metre (3.3 feet) or more in diameter. Good examples are found in the Alps, Germany, Norway, and in the United States.

BASINS FORMED BY FLUVIAL AND MARINE PROCESSES

Fluvial action in several forms can produce lake basins. The most important processes include waterfall action, damming by sediment deposition from a tributary (fluviatile dams), sediment deposition in river deltas, damming by tidal transport of sediments upstream, changes in the configuration of river channels (e.g., oxbow lakes and levee lakes), and solution of subsurface rocks by groundwater.

This last mechanism has produced the well-known formations in the Karst region, in Yugoslavia, which include subterranean and surface cavities and basins in limestone. The term karstic phenomena is applied to similar cases in many parts of the world. Solution lakes in Florida (e.g., Deep Lake) are also of this origin, as are Lünersee and Seewlisee, in the Alps. Other rock types susceptible to solution basin formation include gypsum and halite. Mansfeldersee in Saxony was formed in this manner.

In some coastal areas, longshore marine currents may deposit sufficient sediment to block river outflows. This damming action may be of varying intensity, and it may also occur in lake regions, where such current action causes sediment deposition that leads to the formation of multiple lakes. Accumulation of organic plant material also can result in structures that produce lake basins. Silver Lake, in Nova Scotia, evolved from damming by plant material. Structural formations of coral are another potential cause of damming.

BASINS FORMED BY WIND ACTION, ANIMAL ACTIVITY, AND METEORITES

Wind action may lead to dam or dune construction or erosion and thus can play a role in lake-basin formation. The latter case has been demonstrated in North America. A number of basins in Texas and northward, on the plains east from the Rocky Mountains, are thought to have originated from wind erosion—at least in part. Moses Lake in Washington State was formed by windblown sand that dammed the basin.

Mammals have constructed lake-forming dams. The American beaver is highly skilled at this, and its activities in this connection have established it as a symbol of industriousness. Man has also been busy in this regard and is fully capable of producing lakes that would rival the largest of the more natural variety. Plans once proposed for the damming of the Yukon River in Alaska would, if carried through, result in the formation of a lake larger than Lake Erie in surface area. Other human activities, such as quarrying and mining, also have produced cavities suitable for lake formation.

The last major mechanism of basin formation is that due to meteoritic impact. Meteorite craters are best preserved in arid climates and are often dry for this reason. A few lakes are known in craters, however, including Ungava Lake, in Quebec. In many other cases, it has not been possible to definitely confirm that basins that have the appearance of meteorite craters have, indeed, been produced by meteorite impact. Controversial ones include the bay lakes of southeast North America.

BASIN TOPOGRAPHY

Lakes meet with both the atmosphere and the underlying material of their terrestrial basins and interact with each. The topography and configuration of the lake bottom and the nature of the bottom materials vary considerably. They are of sufficient importance to most lake processes to warrant recognition as basic lake characteristics.

The surface area of a lake can easily be determined by cartographic techniques, but lake-volume determinations require knowledge of lake depths. Throughout the world, lakes important enough to warrant study have been sounded, and many nations have completed comprehensive programs to determine the bathymetry of large numbers of lakes. Lake sounding involves traversing a lake to collect either point or continuous measurements of depth until an accurate survey is made. Modern sounding devices measure the time taken for emitted sound to return after reflection from the bottom, relying on a knowledge of the speed of sound in water. The more sophisticated of these also provide for detection of the depths of stratification in sedimentary materials on the lake bottom. The employment of laser devices from aircraft is a recent development that is based on the transmission of light beams with wavelengths that will penetrate water.

For more practical purposes, lake morphology is a stable characteristic. Shore erosion, sediment deposition and transfer, and other processes, however, including dredging by man, may significantly alter a lake's bottom topography and thus affect navigation, currents, and ecological factors, such as fish spawning grounds.

SEDIMENTS AND SEDIMENTATION

Lake sediments are comprised mainly of clastic material (sediment of clay, silt, and sand sizes), organic debris, chemical precipitates, or combinations of these. The relative abundance of each depends upon the nature of the local drainage basin, the climate, and the relative age of a lake. The sediments of a lake in a glaciated basin, for example, will first receive coarse clastics, then finer clastics, chemical precipitates, and then increasingly large amounts of biological material, including peats and sedges.

Geologists can deduce much about a lake's history and the history of the lake basin and climate from the sedimentary records on its bottom. A sediment core contains such clues as ripple marks caused by current or wave action, carbonaceous layers, and alternations of strata that include cold- and warm-water species of fossils, pollen, and traces of chemicals of human derivation. These data provide the basis for extensive documentation of lake history (paleolimnology). Some well-known historical events, such as major volcanic eruptions, the clearing of North American forests by early settlers as revealed by pollen concentrations, the first extensive use of certain heavy metals by industry, and nuclear explosions, provide reference points in the sediment record.

Many of the materials that are detrimental to the ecology of a lake—e.g., excessive quantities of nutrients, heavy metals, pesticides, oil, and certain bacteria—are deposited in lake sediments by chemical precipitation or the settling of particulate matter. These materials are potentially available for regeneration into the lake water and must be considered in any planning for measures to abate lake pollution. Within the uppermost lake sediments, large volumes of interstitial water are often present. This water may have high concentrations of nutrients and other constituents and enhance the exchange potential with the lake proper.

Clastic Sediments

Waters draining into a lake carry with them much of the suspended sediment that is transported by rivers and streams from the local drainage basin. Current and wave action along the shoreline is responsible for additional erosion and sediment deposition, and some material may be introduced as a result of wind action. Rivers and streams transport material of many different sizes, the largest being rolled along the riverbed (the bed load). When river water enters a lake, its speed diminishes rapidly, bed-load transport ceases, and the suspended load begins to settle to the bottom, the largest sizes first. Lake outlets carry with them only those materials that are too small to have settled out from the inflows or those that have been introduced adjacent to the outflow. Because dynamic processes that keep materials suspended are generally more active near the shore, lake sediments are usually sorted by size. The rocks, pebbles, and coarse sands occur near shore, whereas the finer sands, silts, and muds are, in most cases, found offshore.

Clastic material over most of a lake basin consists principally of silts and clays, especially away from shores and river mouths, where larger material is deposited. Clays exist in a variety of colours, black clays containing large concentrations of organic matter or sulfides and whiter clays usually containing high calcium carbonate concentrations. Other colours, including reds and greens, are known to reflect particular chemical and biological influences.

Organic sediments are derived from plant and animal matter: *förna* is recognizable plant and animal remains, *äfja* finely divided remains in colloidal suspension, and *gyttja* is a deposit formed from *äfja* that has been oxidized. Rapid accumulation of organic matter in still lakes is not uncommon; in the English Lake District, 5 metres (15 feet) of lake sediment of organic origin accumulated over a period of about 8,000 years. Pollen analysis has been used to accurately decipher climatic conditions of the lake in the past.

Varved deposits are the product of an annual cycle of sedimentation; seasonal changes are responsible for the information. Varves are a common feature in many areas and especially so where the land has received meltwaters from ice sheets and glaciers. The deposits consist of alternating layers of fine and coarse sediments.

Coarse clastic materials seldom are larger than boulders (25 cm [10 inches]), and the type of material in sizes larger than silt and clay frequently reveals its source. Materials along lakeshores can in most cases be traced back to a particular eroded source within the local drainage basin, and the distribution of this material provides evidence of the predominant current or wave patterns in the lake.

Volcanic ash is deposited downwind from its source. Ash from volcanic activity during the Pleistocene Epoch can often be dated and used as a stratigraphic marker. Lakes throughout the northwestern United States contain some of the best examples (the Mazama ash), and one deposit in the central United States, called the Pearlette ash deposit, occurs in beds as thick as 3 metres (10 feet).

CHEMICAL PRECIPITATES

The major chemical precipitates in lake systems are calcium, sodium, and magnesium carbonates and dolomite, gypsum, halite, and sulfate salts. Calcium carbonate is deposited as either calcite or aragonite when a lake becomes saturated with calcium and bicarbonate ions. Photosynthesis can also generate precipitation of calcium carbonate, when plant material takes up carbon dioxide and bicarbonate and raises the pH above about 9 (the pH is a measure of the acidity or alkalinity of water. Acid waters have a pH of less than 7, and the pH of alkaline waters range from 7 to 14).

Dolomite deposition occurs in very alkaline lakes when calcium carbonate and magnesium carbonate combine. Recent dolomites have been found in Lake Balqash, in Kazakhstan. In many saline lakes, gypsum deposition has occurred; Lake Eyre, Australia, is estimated to contain more than 4 billion tons of gypsum. For gypsum to be deposited, sulfate, calcium, and hydrogen sulfide must be present in particular concentrations. Hydrogen sulfide occurs in deoxygenated portions of lakes, usually following the depletion of oxygen resulting from decomposition of biological material. Bottom-dwelling organisms are usually absent.

Lakes that contain high concentrations of sodium sulfate are called bitter lakes, and those containing sodium carbonate are called alkali lakes. Soda Lake, California, is estimated to contain nearly 1 million tons of anhydrous sulfate. Magnesium salts of these types are also quite common and can be found in the same sediments as the sodium salts. Other salts of importance occurring in lake sediments include borates, nitrates, and potash. Small quantities of borax are found in various lakes throughout the world. Lakes with high alkalinity levels, such as Mono Lake in California, can still support some forms of life.

The gradual increase of sediment thickness through time may threaten the very existence of a lake. When a lake becomes shallow enough to support the growth of bottom-attached plants, these may accelerate the extinction of a lake. In several European countries, steps are being taken to restore lakes threatened by choking plant growth. Lake Hornborgasjön, Sweden, long prized as a national wildlife refuge, became the subject of an investigation in 1967. Lake Trummen, also in Sweden, was treated by dredging its upper sediments. In Switzerland, Lake Wiler (Wilersee) was treated by the removal of water just above the sediments during stagnation periods.

LAKE WATERS

Lake waters are sites of significant chemical and physical activity. Lake waters contain chemical compounds involved in plant and animal respiration. The availability of some chemicals, such as orthophosphates and nitrates, limit the growth of plants in lake ecosystems. Lake waters also serve as reservoirs of heat. The differences in seasonal heating, along with the special density characteristics of water, affect how energy is exchanged with the atmosphere and transferred between layers of water in the basin.

CHEMICAL COMPOSITION

Although the chemical composition of lakes varies considerably throughout the world, owing to the varying chemistry of the erosion products of different lake basins, in most cases the principal constituents are quite similar. Human influences also have contributed substantially to the chemical composition of lakes, and, although industrial effluents vary somewhat from lake to lake, many of the chemical effects of human activities are similar throughout the world. Another source in the chemical balance of lakes is the dissolved and suspended material contained in precipitation. Again, human activities have been in large part responsible for steadily increasing concentrations of this input.

SALINITY, NUTRIENTS, AND OXYGEN

Salinity is the total concentration of the ions present in lake water and is usually computed from the sodium, potassium, magnesium, calcium, carbonate, silicate, and halide concentrations. Several important bodies of inland waters, often called inland seas, have very high salinities. Great Salt Lake, in Utah, has a salinity of about 200,000 milligrams per litre, as compared with Lake Superior's value of about 75 and an estimated mean for all rivers of 100 to 150. These ions are steadily introduced to lakes from rivers and rainwater, where they concentrate because of the evaporative loss of relatively pure water.

Where inflowing rivers erode igneous rocks, lake salinity values are relatively low, but, where soluble salts are available for erosion, salinities are relatively high. In general, it has been found that, of the cations (positively charged ions), calcium concentrations are highest, followed by magnesium, sodium, and potassium, in that order. Among the major anions (negatively charged ions), carbonate is generally the most abundant, followed by sulfate and chloride.

Other inorganic ions, though present in smaller concentrations, are of great importance. In particular, the nutrients (especially phosphate, nitrate, and silicate), heavy metals (e.g., mercury, manganese, copper, lead), and polychlorinated hydrocarbons (DDT, for example) have attracted recent interest because of their role in ecological problems. Although sources of nutrients and mercury exist that are not directly related to human activities, budget studies and studies of the historical records available in sediment cores clearly reveal the great impact of human disposal of these constituents in lakes. Rainfall and dry fallout are small but significant chemical inputs to lakes. The release of gases and particulate matter into the atmosphere from factories and similar sources has increased dramatically in recent years, with consequent alterations in the chemistry of rainwater. It has been estimated, for example, that 16,000 tons of nitrogen, about 8 percent of the total from all sources, is introduced annually to Lake Erie from atmospheric action.

The substance of most interest in lakes is oxygen. Once introduced to the lake water, its concentration is subject to factors within the water. Biological production (photosynthesis) releases oxygen into the water, while biological decay consumes it. Various chemical reactions within the lake system also affect the concentration of dissolved oxygen. The main source is the passage of oxygen through the air-water interface, which is affected principally by the lake temperatures; at low temperatures the partial pressure of dissolved oxygen in water is reduced. Consequently, during cold seasons, especially when vertical mixing is greatly enhanced because of a lack of thermal structure and increased wind stirring, lakes are replenished with oxygen. In the warmer seasons, although surface waters may remain more or less saturated and even supersaturated, the concentrations are lower. Beneath the surface, oxygen consumption through biological decay may cause serious depletion. Oxygen depletion also occurs near the bottom because of processes at the mud-water interface, many of which are still inadequately explained.

In winter months, a rapid formation of ice or the establishment of strong winter thermal stratification may significantly inhibit the replenishment of oxygen. Where ice cover lasts for long periods, a loss of oxygen at the mud-water interface may have repercussions for the whole lake, particularly if density currents cause significant vertical transport.

In tropical regions, where the winter replenishment mechanism (turnover) is absent, there is great reliance on the occasional occurrence of cold spells or on significant nighttime cooling to promote oxygen replenishment. Deep lakes in these regions are often anoxic (lacking in oxygen) in the deeper portions.

At any particular time, lake waters or waters entering a lake may have a biological or chemical potential for oxygen utilization. Measurements of this are termed BOD (biological oxygen demand) or COD (chemical oxygen demand). These concepts are used as partial indicators of the quality of waters being introduced to a lake.

Lakes that have a vertical salinity gradient strong enough to prevent winter turnover will usually be deoxygenated at depths where the vertical diffusion of oxygen is less than the oxygen demand. Such lakes are termed meromictic.

CARBON DIOXIDE

Another gaseous substance of great importance that is exchanged with the atmosphere at the surface is carbon dioxide. Photosynthesis requires the presence of carbon dioxide, and it is released during biological breakdown.

Carbon dioxide is very soluble in lake water; it forms carbonic acid, which dissociates and raises the concentration of hydrogen ions (lowering the pH). The relative proportions of bicarbonate, carbonate, and free carbon dioxide depend upon the pH. At high values of pH, carbonate ions will predominate; at low values, free carbon dioxide and carbonic acid will predominate.

Various carbonates (particularly sodium, calcium, potassium, and magnesium) are important to the carbon dioxide system. Increased pressure of carbon dioxide in the system increases the solubilities of these carbonates. In some cases, photosynthetic activity results in precipitation of certain carbonates. The entire carbon dioxide system and its behaviour at various pH values is very complex but can be interpreted from historical knowledge of lake sediments.

In waters that are neither very acidic (pH much less than 7) nor very basic (pH much greater than 7 but less than 14), the carbon dioxide system serves as a buffer, because, within limits, a change in pH will cause a shift within the system that ultimately serves to offset the pH change. Consequently, most lakes have a pH between 6 and 8. Some volcanic lakes are extremely acid, however, with pH values below 4, and some lakes with very high pH values, such as Lake Nakuru, Kenya, also occur in nature.

Sulfates, Nitrates, and Phosphates

Sulfate usually occurs as a principal ion in lake waters. Under anaerobic conditions in which bacteria persist in the oxidation of biological material, hydrogen sulfide is produced. When anoxic conditions exist in the deep waters just above the sediments, and the water is acidic enough to precipitate the iron present, hydrogen sulfide occurs. The characteristic and unpleasant odour of this gas is often popularly identified with the "death" of a lake. Big Soda Lake, Nevada, is extremely rich in this substance.

Nitrogen and its various compounds form another complex system in lakes, appearing as free nitrogen in solution, organic compounds, ammonia, nitrite, and nitrate. Sources of nitrogen compounds include influents to the lake (the most important source), fixation in the lake, and precipitation. Losses are experienced mainly through effluents but also by denitrification, sediment formation, and loss to the atmosphere.

Orthophosphate and various organic phosphates are the most important phosphorous compounds in lakes.

Phosphates and nitrates are heavily consumed in the upper portion of lakes during periods of high productivity of phytoplankton. Increased concentrations occur in deeper portions due to decay of falling biological material and regeneration from the sediments, especially during anoxic conditions or stormy periods in shallow lakes. As limiting nutrients in many lake productivity cycles, phosphates and nitrates are often identified as controllable elements in situations where abatement is necessary to control eutrophication. Carbon is also a necessary constituent for production and in some cases can be the limiting component. Because carbon is less easily controlled and not often limiting, however, phosphates are most frequently named as substances to be reduced in effluents from industry and municipalities.

Silica also is present in lake waters, and, as with the other nutrients, it is introduced in influents and to some extent from the sediments. The production of diatom blooms is a major process for reducing silicate concentrations. Within this context, silica can also be regarded as a limiting nutrient.

THERMAL PROPERTIES

Pure water freezes at 0 °C (32 °F), boils at 100 °C (212 °F), and has a latent heat of evaporation of 539.55 calories per gram, a latent heat of sublimation (ice) of 679 calories per gram, and a specific heat of 1.01 calories per gram, per °C, at 0 °C. The temperature of maximum density of water at atmospheric pressure occurs at 3.94 °C (39.09 °F). At the freezing point, ice has a lower density than water. For natural waters with high salinities, such as the oceans and inland seas, each of the values above is significantly altered. In most lakes, however, these numbers are quite representative.

EUTROPHICATION

Historically, aquatic systems have been classified as oligotrophic or eutrophic. Oligotrophic waters are poorly fed by the nutrients nitrogen and phosphorus and have low concentrations of these constituents. There is thus low production of organic matter by photosynthesis in such waters. By contrast, eutrophic waters are well supplied with nutrients and generally have high concentrations of nitrogen and phosphorus and, correspondingly, large concentrations of plankton owing to high biological productivity. The waters of such aquatic systems are usually murky, and lakes and coastal marine systems may be oxygen-depleted at depth.

The process of eutrophication is defined as high biological productivity resulting from increased input of nutrients or organic matter into aquatic systems. For lakes, this increased biological productivity usually leads to decreased lake volume because of the accumulation of organic detritus. Natural eutrophication occurs as aquatic systems fill in with organic matter; it is distinct from cultural eutrophication, which is caused by human intervention. The latter is characteristic of aquatic systems that have been artificially enriched by excess nutrients and organic matter from sewage, agriculture, and industry. Naturally eutrophic lakes may produce 75–250 grams of carbon per square metre per year, whereas those lakes experiencing eutrophication because of human activities can support 75–750 grams per square metre per year. Commonly, culturally eutrophic aquatic systems may exhibit extremely low oxygen concentrations in bottom waters. This is particularly true of stratified systems, as, for instance, lakes during summer where concentrations of molecular oxygen may reach levels of less than about one milligram per litre — a threshold for various biological and chemical processes.

Aquatic systems may change from oligotrophic to eutrophic, or the rate of eutrophication of a natural eutrophic system may be accelerated by the addition of nutrients and organic matter due to human activities. The process of cultural eutrophication, however, can be reversed if the excess nutrient and organic matter supply is shut off.

Not only do freshwater aquatic systems undergo cultural eutrophication, but coastal marine systems also may be affected by this process. On a global scale, the input by rivers of organic matter to the oceans today is twice the input in prehuman times, and the flux of nitrogen, together with that of phosphorus, has more than doubled. This excess loading of carbon, nitrogen, and phosphorus is leading to cultural eutrophication of marine systems. In several polluted eastern U.S. estuaries and in some estuaries of western Europe (e.g., the Scheldt of Belgium and the Netherlands), all of the dissolved silica brought into the estuarine waters by rivers is removed by phytoplankton growth (primarily diatoms) resulting from excess fluxes of nutrients and organic matter. In the North Sea, there is now a deficiency of silica and an excess of nitrogen and phosphorus, which in turn has led to a decrease in diatom productivity and an increase in cyanobacteria productivity—a biotic change brought about by cultural eutrophication.

The density of water increases at pressures above one atmosphere (the pressure at sea level). Thus, pure water at 10 °C (50 °F) has a density of 0.9995 at one atmosphere and 1.0037 at the pressure existing at a lake depth of 1,000 metres (3,000 feet). Water raised from great depths to conditions of lower pressure experiences adiabatic cooling (without significant heat exchange with surrounding water), but there are very few lakes in which this factor can be of much significance.

VERTICAL MIXING AND OVERTURN

It is useful to know how the temperature of maximum density changes with depth (e.g., from 3.94 °C [39 °F] at the surface to 3.39 °C at 500 metres depth [38.10 °F at 1,500 feet]). The fact that the temperature of maximum density of most lake waters is close to 4 °C (39 °F), whereas ice forms at temperatures close to 0 °C in response to surface cooling, vertical mixing takes place. When density increases with depth, the lake is said to be stable. Unstable conditions exist when density decreases with depth. Cooling at the surface to temperatures below 4 °C establishes stability based on a negative thermocline (a positive thermocline is a vertical decrease in temperature with depth), because density will increase with depth. Ice then forms at the surface, enabling liquid water to exist beneath the ice in lakes, unless they are shallow enough to freeze to the bottom.

During the warming season, after ice has melted, heating increases the density of the surface waters, causing them to sink until stability is achieved. When surface heating proceeds above the temperature of maximum density, this process ceases, and the vertical thermal structure maintains and strengthens its stable condition, based on a positive thermocline. Turnovers tend to be seasonal.

Mixing due to cooling or warming processes that increase the density of surface waters sufficiently to cause them to sink results in what is termed circulation, or overturn, of lake waters. Lakes that cool to below 4 °C in winter experience two turnover periods, as just described, and are called dimictic lakes. Most lakes in temperate regions fall into this category. Lakes that do not cool to below 4 °C undergo overturn only once per year and are called warm monomictic. Lakes that do not warm to above 4 °C also experience only one overturn period per year and are called cold monomictic. There are many examples of the former, including lakes in the tropical regions and generally as far north as about 40°. The cold monomictic type, however, is less common but can be found at high latitudes and at high altitudes (in the Alps, for example).

All the types described that circulate at least once throughout are called holomictic. It is possible, however, for lakes to be stable despite the thermal processes that normally induce overturn owing to the existence of a positive salinity gradient with depth (chemocline). This type is called meromictic, and, in those cases where stability is permanent in at least part of the lake, the deep waters do not experience overturn and consequently are deoxygenated. Three principal origins of meromixis have been recognized. Ectogenic meromixis results from either the intrusion of seawater into a lake, as in the case of flooding from an unusually high sea level (e.g., Hemmelsdorfersee, in Germany), or the introduction of fresh water through land drainage and precipitation to a saline lake (e.g., Soda Lake, Nevada). Crenogenic meromixis is due to the introduction of saline water by springs, and biogenic meromixis is due to the uptake of salts from the lake sediments. North American examples include Lake Mary, Wisconsin, and Sodon Lake, Michigan.

A strong vertical salinity gradient that exists in the upper portion of a lake will affect the thermal structure by inhibiting the downward mixing of heat. In holomictic lakes, however, the downward mixing of heat due primarily to wind action usually compresses or concentrates the thermocline until it essentially separates an upper layer (epilimnion) from a lower layer (hypolimnion), each possessing weak or nonexistent vertical thermal gradients. The thermocline normally begins to grow at the beginning of the warming season. As summer passes and autumn commences, it intensifies and deepens. The onset of the cooling sees the beginning of the decay of the thermocline from above, although it usually continues to deepen until it is completely destroyed. The process just described is commonly found in lakes in temperate regions and is a seasonal phenomenon. During any period of strong warming, one or more shallower thermoclines may be observed to develop and move downward to the seasonal thermocline.

THE HEAT BUDGET OF LAKES

The heat budget of a lake includes several major factors: net incoming solar radiation, net exchange of long-wave radiation emitted by the lake surface and the atmosphere, transfer of sensible heat at the surface interface, and latent-heat processes. Those processes that are usually of much smaller importance include net inflow and outflow of heat advected by streamflow, precipitation, and ground-water flow, conduction from terrestrial heat flow, and dissipation of kinetic energy. In some cases, however, river inflow may be of more importance, such as where flow is from a nearby glacier or where the volume inflow is a significant fraction of the lake volume. Within a large lake the heat-budget considerations for a particular location must also take into account the local advection of heat within the lake by currents.

Incoming solar energy varies seasonally and with the latitude and is greatly influenced by cloud cover. The fraction that is reflected away from the lake surface depends upon the solar angle, the turbidity of the atmosphere, and the wave state, or surface roughness. In middle latitudes this ranges from about 6 percent in summer months to about 14 percent in winter.

The amount of radiation emitted by the lake surface is proportional to the fourth power of the surface temperature, whereas the radiation emitted by the clouds and atmosphere overlying the lake depends primarily upon the amount and height of the clouds and the temperature and moisture content of the atmosphere near the lake surface.

The fluxes of sensible heat and moisture at the lake surface are of great importance yet are still poorly understood. They depend upon the vertical gradients of temperature and vapour pressure above the water, respectively, and upon the factors that influence the transfer processes, such as wind and atmospheric stability. The transfer of sensible heat may be either into or out of the lake surface, usually on a seasonal basis but also sometimes on a diurnal basis. It is also possible but less likely for condensation to occur on a lake surface.

Heat flow through the bottom of lakes is normally of small significance, but exceptions exist. In a very deep lake where low rates of heating are important, such as Lake Baikal, Russia, the results may be detectable. In some ice-covered lakes where other sources of heating are small, heat flux through sediments also has been shown to be significant.

The dissipation of wind energy that has been transferred to water movements is quite insignificant, as is the effect of heat transfer due to chemical and photosynthetic processes.

In latitudes and altitudes where ice is a factor, the latent heats of fusion and of evaporation of ice must also be considered within any heat-budget considerations. Heat-balance studies have been performed for lakes that are always ice covered. Solar radiation is often an important factor where ice thickness and consistency permits penetration. The heat balance of the ice is often difficult to assess, as long-wave radiation and evaporation factors are not easily measured and are very important. The exchange of sensible heat may not be large during summer months in these cases but is likely to be significant in the colder months. Several lakes that are ice covered have been shown to be meromictic; two examples are Lake Tuborg, Ellesmere Island and Lake Bonney, Antarctica.

Heat-balance measurements or estimates have been made for many lakes throughout the world. Results show that the difference between the highest and lowest heat content for each lake varies from around 5,000 calories per square centimetre for high and low latitudes to around 45,000 calories for some midlatitude lakes.

The relative importance of each of the major terms of the heat budget is shown by data for two North American lakes: Lake Ontario, a large, deep, middle-latitude lake; and Lake Hefner, a relatively small, shallow lake in

Oklahoma. The energy unit frequently employed is the langley (one gram calorie per square centimetre), and the figures given are approximate monthly means of langleys per day. Net solar radiation input to Lake Ontario varies from 80 to 600 (Lake Hefner varies from 200 to 600), midwinter to midsummer. Net losses due to long-wave radiation from Lake Ontario are nearly 100 throughout the year (Lake Hefner varies from 100 to 200). Evaporation losses for Lake Ontario vary from 250 in midwinter to slightly negative values in early summer (Lake Hefner varies from 450 in late summer to 150 in spring). Conduction of heat from the surface of Lake Ontario varies from 250 in winter to about minus 100 in summer (Lake Hefner varies considerably from 80 to -80 for the same time interval).

HEAT TRANSFER

Heat added to a lake at the surface is usually mixed mechanically downward as a result of wind action. This process keeps the upper portion of a lake relatively uniform thermally. Consequently, a thermal gradient (thermocline) becomes established between the upper mixed layer (epilimnion) and the deep portion of the lake (hypolimnion). In shallow lakes or shallow portions of large lakes, the thermocline will eventually intercept the lake bottom so that no hypolimnion exists. Normally, as the heating season progresses, the thermocline intensifies and deepens. Secondary thermoclines may develop in the epilimnion, and these will migrate downward to the main seasonal thermocline. On very warm, still days, a thin surface layer may store heat before a mixing episode transfers heat downward. When the cooling season commences, the mixing that tends to destroy the thermocline is enhanced by vertical convection. If the cooling continues until the entire thermocline is eliminated, the lake becomes essentially isothermal and no longer exhibits the characteristics of a two-layered system.

When a lake is stratified, the most important process for downward transfer of heat to the hypolimnion is through eddy conduction. The coefficient of eddy conductivity is determined empirically and varies substantially from lake to lake. Mixing processes are generally more active in coastal areas, so that isotherms can be expected to slope downward toward shore. In large, relatively unprotected lakes, wind stress at the surface causes convergence or divergence or both of shallow waters along coastlines. Isotherms will slant upward toward the shore, and hypolimnion water may even become exposed at the surface. These occurrences are of great importance with regard to the distribution of heat within stratified lakes.

Heat introduced to lakes in large quantities, as a waste product of cooling processes in power-generating plants and other industrial concerns, is presently viewed with some concern as a pollutant, especially in small lakes. If the heat is injected at the surface it will spread initially according to the momentum of the influent and the speed and direction of ambient surface currents. When the initial momentum is sufficiently dissipated, the heat will spread mainly as a consequence of turbulent mixing processes. Throughout these events, substantial losses of heat to the atmosphere may occur, so that the full effects of the thermal input are not borne solely by the lake. Temperature values at the surface, adjacent to the influent-heat source, may be raised to a very high level—as much as several centigrade degrees. Under certain conditions fish-activity tolerances may be exceeded, and undesirable algae and plankton production may be stimulated.

If waste heat is not released at the surface but is diffused over a large depth range or injected at depth, the large local-surface-temperature problem is avoided. Losses to the atmosphere in this case, however, are also greatly reduced, and the net heat input to the lake as a whole is much greater. Over a long period, this may prove to be more detrimental to the general ecology than near-surface injection.

USES AND ABUSES OF LAKES

In today's industrial societies, requirements for water—much of which is derived from lakes—include its use for dilution and removal of municipal and industrial wastes, for cooling purposes, for irrigation, for power generation, and for local recreation and aesthetic displays. Obviously, these requirements vary considerably among regions, climates, and countries.

In another vein, it is convenient to use water to dilute liquid and some solid wastes to concentrations that are not intolerable to the elements of society that must be exposed to the effluent or wish to use it. The degree of dilution that may be acceptable varies from situation to situation and is often in dispute. In some cases, dilution is used purely to facilitate transport of the wastes to purification facilities. The water may then be made available for reuse.

Lake water is also used extensively for cooling purposes. Although this water may not be affected chemically, its change in thermal quality may be detrimental to the environment into which it is disposed, either directly, by affecting fish health or functions, or indirectly, by causing excessive plant production and ultimate deoxygenation due to biological decay. Both fossil- and nuclear-fuelled power plants are major users of cooling water. Steel mills and various chemical plants also require large quantities.

ECONOMY AND ECOLOGY

Concern with thermal pollution of surface waters is concentrated principally on rivers and small lakes. With power requirements in modern societies increasing by about 7 percent per year, however, some apprehension has been expressed about the future thermal loading of even the largest lakes. It was predicted that thermal inputs to each of the North American Great Lakes will increase by nearly 11 times during the last three decades of the 20th century. In terms of energy to be disposed in this fashion, the numbers are staggeringly large. These lakes have such large volumes, however, and such large surface areas (from which much of the heat goes into the atmosphere) that there is some question about the nature and magnitude of the actual effects.

The economic importance of waterways as communication links is enormous. In the earliest times, when travel by many societies was substantially by water, travel routes became established that resulted in relationships between cultural factors and surface hydrology networks. Today, river and lake systems serve as communication links and play an important role in shipping because of the large cargo capacities of merchant vessels and the still fairly uncongested condition of inland waterways. Oceanic shipping lanes play the major role, but river and lake systems, which link inland ports with the oceans, have been key factors in the rates of economic growth of many large inland ports.

Commercial fisheries and other food industries reap great harvests from the major lakes of the world. The quality of the fish catch has steadily decreased, however, as a result of pollution in many lakes, with the more desirable species becoming less plentiful and the less desirable species gradually dominating the total. Other commercial harvests from lakes include waterfowl, fur-bearing mammals, and some plant material, such as rice.

Each of the uses described has associated with it the means for abuse of the very characteristics of lakes that make them desirable. Wise management of natural resources has never been humankind's forte. Municipalities and industries have polluted lakes chemically and thermally, the shipping that plies large inland water bodies leaves oil and other refuse in its wake, water used for irrigation often contains chemical residues from fertilizers and biocides when it is returned to lakes, and the populace that so desperately demands clean bodies of water for its recreation often ignores basic sanitary and antipollution practices, to the ultimate detriment of the waters enjoyed.

Fishermen hauling in the day's catch. Pollution threatens the viability of the world's lakes as prime fishing grounds. Medioimages/Photodisc/ Getty Images

PROBLEMS AND EFFECTS

Among the major problems affecting the optimum utilization and conservation of lake waters are eutrophication (aging processes), chemical and biological poisoning, and decreases in water volumes. In the former case, discussed in more detail later, the enrichment of lakes with various nutrients supports biological productivity to an extent in which the ultimate death and decay of biological material places an excessive demand on the oxygen content, resulting in oxygen depletion in the worst cases. Phosphates and nitrates are two of the types of nutrients that are most important in this connection, particularly since they are often introduced in critical quantities in waste effluents from human sources. Other examples of chemical pollution of lakes include the introduction of DDT and other pesticides and heavy metals such as mercury. Bacteriological contamination of lake waters resulting in levels that constitute a hazard to health is another common result of disregard for the environment.

Water-quantity problems are complex, being related to natural vagaries of supply and levels of consumptive utilization of water. In the latter case, the percentage of water returned to the source after utilization varies with the use. The largest losses are due to actual water diversions and processes that result in evaporative losses. The use of large quantities of lake water for cooling purposes by industry and utilities, for example, may raise lake temperatures near the effluents sufficiently to cause increased evaporation. The use of certain types of cooling towers results in even larger losses. Some of the water evaporated will stay within the lake basin, but some will be lost from it.

Another example of this type of loss is connected with the possible application of weather-modification techniques to alleviate the heavy lake-effect snowfalls experienced along the lee shores of large lakes in intermediate latitudes. Redistribution of precipitation always raises the possibility of redistribution of water among various basins.

Lake-effect snowfall is just one example of the influence of lakes on local climate. The ability of large bodies of water to store heat during heating periods and to lose it more gradually than the adjacent landmasses during cooling periods results in a modifying influence on the climate. Because of this propensity, a lake cools air passing over it in summer and warms air passing over it in winter. Consequently, the predominantly downwind side of a lake is more influenced by the ameliorating effects of a lake.

In most instances, moisture is also passed to the atmosphere. In summer, lake cooling serves to stabilize the air mass, but winter heating tends to decrease stability. The moisture-laden, unstable winter flows off lakes produce so-called snowbelts, which affect downwind cities. The snowbelts are usually of limited extent, often within about a kilometre (0.62 mile) of the lake shore.

CHAPTER 2
LAKE HYDRAULICS

The movement of water within lake basins is facilitated by several forces. Currents caused by winds and water inflows and outflows are the primary movers of water in lakes. However, surface waves and seiches can also affect water flow. The movement of water powers the processes of erosion and deposition that affect the bottom morphology of lake basins. In addition, the maintenance of the basin's water level depends on balancing inputs from groundwater, precipitation, and other sources with outflows from evaporation, streams that allow water to exit the basin, and other sinks.

CURRENTS

The principal forces acting to initiate water movements in lakes are those due to hydraulic gradients, wind stress, and factors that cause horizontal or vertical density gradients. Lake water movement is usually classified as being turbulent.

Hydraulic effects are frequently the result of inflows and outflows of water. These may be substantial and continuous or weak and sporadic. In terms of the ratio of the volume of the inflow or outflow to the lake volume, the latter is the most frequently observed situation.

The stress of wind moving over the lake surface causes a transport of water within the lake, as well as the movement of energy downwind through the mechanism of surface waves. The wind is therefore one of the most important external forces on a lake. It can be relatively consistent in speed and direction, or it can be highly variable in either or both.

PRESSURE GRADIENTS

Water movements can occur as a result of internal pressure gradients and from density gradients caused by variations in temperature, sediment concentration, or the concentration of dissolved substances. Surface water in lakes can become denser than underlying water either by cooling or heating, because the temperature of maximum density for pure lake water is about 4 °C (39 °F). Water entering a lake from rivers with a high concentration of dissolved substances will sink to a lake level of similar density. These movements are both horizontal and vertical, but the net effect is downward, if not vertical, motion.

Horizontal pressure gradients can result from many different processes that act to produce density gradients. One example is the situation of solar heating in a shallow nearshore region, where the heat is committed to the warming of a relatively small volume of water. This produces a water of lower density than the near-surface water of an adjacent deep region, where the heat is spread throughout a greater volume. Consequently, the pressure gradient force will act to move the warmer water offshore and to replace it from below with cooler water.

Lake currents are the result of complex interactions of forces, but in many cases a small number of particular forces dominate. In the case of horizontal flow in the absence of horizontal pressure gradients, assuming no friction, water set in motion will curve to the right in the Northern Hemisphere because the Earth rotates from west to east. This effect is called the Coriolis force, and it will continue to influence water motion until there is a balance with the centrifugal force. This movement causes free-floating markers to move in an elliptical manner with a period that depends upon the latitude. In Lake Ontario, for example, it is about 17 hours. Where a dominating pressure gradient exists, the balance of the pressure-gradient force with the Coriolis force results in the so-called geostrophic flow, at right angles to the pressure gradient, with low pressure on the left (Northern Hemisphere). These conditions are most nearly realized only in very large lakes and in the oceans.

In those small lakes where hydraulic effects dominate, steady flow conditions may be achieved through balance with friction. This situation is commonly encountered in rivers, and relationships exist between mean current speed and the slope and mean depth of the river or narrow lake. These are called gradient currents and occur following situations where the wind or atmosphere pressure gradient causes a tilting of the lake surface (denivellation). In cases where the Coriolis force is a significant factor, the flow down a lake will tend to move toward the right (in the Northern Hemisphere). The development of a deeper countercurrent to the left will occur to compensate for the piling up of water on the right side.

Horizontal pressure gradients will be important in lakes where there are significant inflows of water with markedly different density from ambient lake density or where significant differential surface heating occurs.

WIND STRESS

Currents resulting from wind stress are the most common in lakes. Considerable research is still underway into the mechanism of transfer of wind momentum to water momentum. The stress on the lake is proportional to some power of wind speed, usually taken to be 2, although it evidently varies with wind speed, wave conditions, and atmospheric stability. In large, deep lakes, away from the boundaries, where wind-stress effects may be balanced by Coriolis-force effects, theory suggests that the surface current will move in a direction 45° to the right of the wind and that deeper currents are progressively weaker and directed farther to the right. The depth at which flow is opposite to the wind direction is effectively the depth below which there is no influence from the wind. This depth, designated D, can theoretically occur at about 100 metres (300 feet) in large, deep, midlatitude lakes. Observations show varying degrees of fidelity to theory because of complications from coastal effects and thermal stratification.

In coastal regions, if water depth is a significant fraction of or greater than D, winds blowing parallel to the shore will transport water either onshore or offshore. In the latter case, where the coast is to the left of the wind flow (Northern Hemisphere), the water driven offshore is replaced by cooler, deeper water (upwelling).

INTERNAL WAVES AND LANGMUIR CIRCULATION

Under stratified conditions a strong thermocline will essentially separate a lake into two layers. Shearing forces that develop between these layers cause a motion, termed internal waves, that may serve to directly dissipate a substantial portion of a lake's kinetic energy and act as a coupling between motion in the epilimnion and hypolimnion. A great range of periodicities is observed in the oscillations of the thermoclines, particularly in large lakes. Internal seiches, which are responsible for relatively long-period internal waves, are discussed later.

A small-scale circulation phenomenon that has aroused considerable attention on lakes is Langmuir circulation. On windy days, parallel "streaks" can be observed to develop on the water surface and exhibit continuity for some distance. These streaks may be caused by convergence zones where surface froth and debris collect.

Langmuir circulation thus appears to be a relatively organized mixing mechanism wherein sinking occurs at the streaks and upwelling occurs between the streaks. Under favourable circumstances, this appears to be a key process for mixing heat downward in lakes.

SURFACE WAVES

Wind blowing over a calm lake surface first produces an effect that may appear as a widely varying and fluctuating ruffling of the surface. The first wave motion to develop is relatively regular, consisting of small, uniformly developed waves called capillary waves. These are quite transient, dissipating rapidly if the wind dies away or developing to the more commonly observed and more persistent gravity waves.

Energy will be continually fed to the waves by the frictional drag of the air moving over the water and by the direct force of the wind on the upwind face of the waves. The latter effect occurs only while the waves move more slowly than the wind. Pressure differences at the air–water interface also contribute energy to surface waves. Energy losses occur due mainly to turbulence in the water and, to a smaller extent, to the effects of viscosity.

Waves will continue to grow as long as there is a net addition of energy to them. Their height will increase as a function of wind speed and duration and the distance over which it blows (fetch). Most lakes are so small that fetch considerations are unimportant. Studies in larger lakes, however, have shown that the height of the highest waves are related to the fetch. In these lakes, waves as high as several metres are common, although waves of about seven metres (23 feet) are the highest to be expected. Wave heights in a given portion of a lake may vary considerably, due to interactions that suppress some waves and amplify others. As waves develop, their lengths increase, even after their height has stopped increasing. The phenomenon of swell, commonly observed in the oceans, is not truly realized, even in the largest lakes.

Waves travel in the same direction as the wind that generated them and at right angles to their crests. If they meet a solid object rather than a sloping beach, much of their energy will be reflected. If they enter shallow water obliquely, they are refracted. Wave speed, for waves longer than four times the depth of the water, is approximately equal to the square root of the product of the depth and the gravitational acceleration. For waves in relatively deep water, the wave speed is proportional to the square root of the wavelength.

Waves crest and roll across Lake Superior, in the United States, on a stormy day. Wind creates waves and determines the direction in which they travel.
Anne Rippy/The Image Bank/Getty Images

As wave height increases, the sharpening of the wave crest may result in instability and a breaking off of the crest, a process hastened by the wind. This results in the familiar whitecaps. Waves that run ashore break up in surf. The wave height first decreases slightly, then increases, and the speed decreases, and eventually the wave form disappears as it crumbles into breakers. These can be plunging forms, in which the top curls right over the forward face, or of the spilling type, in which the crest spills down the forward face. A particular wave may break several times before reaching shore.

SEICHES

If a denivellation, or tilting of a lake's surface, occurs as a result of a persistent wind stress or atmospheric pressure gradient, the cessation of the external forcing mechanism will result in a flow of water to restore the lake level. The flow would be periodic and uniform with depth, except for the damping effects of the lake-bottom friction and internal turbulence. Because of this, each successive tilt of the lake surface in the opposite direction occurs at a level slightly less than the previous one. The oscillation proceeds, moving the water back and forth until damping levels the water or until wind and pressure effect another tilt. This process is seiching; the lake oscillation is a seiche. The basic seiche has a single node, but harmonics of the oscillation occur, with several nodes being possible.

The period of the uninodal seiche can be estimated from a formula that equates it to twice the length in the direction of the tilt, divided by the square root of the product of the mean lake depth and the gravitational acceleration.

Seiches have been noted, recorded, and studied for hundreds of years. Lake Geneva in Switzerland, which has an observed uninodal period of about 74 minutes and a binodal period of about 35 minutes, was one of the first lakes to be studied in connection with seiching. The observed uninodal periods of Loch Treig and Loch Earn, Scotland; Lago di Garda, Italy; Lake Vetter, Sweden; and Lake Erie, North America, are approximately 9, 14.5, 43, 179, and 880 minutes, respectively.

Long, relatively narrow lakes that are exposed to a predominance of wind flow along their major axes are most likely to exhibit so-called longitudinal seiches. Transverse seiching can occur across the narrower dimension of a lake. That observed in Lake Geneva, for example, has a period of about 10 minutes.

The height of the denivellation depends upon the strength and duration of the forcing mechanism, as well as on the lake size and dimensions. In small lakes, level changes of a few centimetres are common, whereas, in the Great Lakes, intense storms can produce changes as great as two metres (seven feet). If the disturbance causing the tilting moves across the lake at close to the speed of the shallow-water wave speed, a profound amplification can occur, with possible disastrous consequences.

In addition, seiches can be caused by the pull of other nearby celestial bodies, such as the Sun and Moon, or occur as the result of changes in heating with depth. True tides that result from the gravitational effects of the Moon and Sun are rarely measurable in lakes, but small values of tidal components occasionally have been discerned. In contrast, internal seiching results from thermal stratification. The layers separated by the thermoclines oscillate relative to one another. Observed uninodal periods for Loch Earn, Lake Geneva, Lake Baikal, and Cayuga Lake (New York) are approximately 16, 96, 900 (binodal), and 65 hours, respectively.

Because hypolimnion water is very different from epilimnion water with regard to both thermal and biological characteristics, the massive movements of water and the turbulent exchanges that can occur during internal seiching are very important. Substantial portions of the bottom of shallow lakes can experience periodic alternation of exposure to hypolimnetic and epilimnetic water, and hypolimnetic water can be periodically exposed to the surface.

THE EFFECTS OF WAVE AND CURRENT ACTION

In a lake's early stages of existence, its shore is most susceptible to changes from wave and current action. As these changes occur, there is a tendency over time to an equilibrium condition—a balance between form and processes that depends upon the nature of the materials present (e.g., the size of sand and gravel present). The effectiveness of waves in the erosion process depends in part upon the depth and slope of the lake bottom. Where the shore consists of a sheer cliff adjacent to deep water, wave energy will be reflected away without much erosional effect. The refraction of waves in zones of irregular coastline tends to concentrate wave energy at some locations and dilute it in others. Thus, features extended out into the lake will receive more wave energy, and the tendency is to smooth out an irregular coastline. Other net effects of shore erosion are an increase in the surface area of a lake and a reduction in its mean depth.

As erosion takes place, the distribution of erosion products results in transport of finer material offshore. The resulting terrace is called the beach in its above-water manifestation and the littoral shelf where it is below water. Landward, beyond the beach, a wave-cut cliff is usually found. The steeper slope that often separates the littoral shelf from the benthos (bottom) zone in the central part of the lake is called the step-off by some limnologists.

Water movement directed at an angle to the coastline will result in the generation of currents along the shore. Erosion products will then be transported down the coast and may be deposited in locations where transport energy is dissipated due to movement around a bend or past an obstruction. A buildup of such material is called a spit. If a bay becomes completely enclosed in this way, the spit is called a bar.

Water in very shallow lakes that are subjected to strong winds may be piled against the lee shore to such an extent that countercurrents will develop from along the lee shore around each side of the lake. The cutting effects of these currents are known as end-current erosion and may characteristically alter the shape of a lake frequently subjected to winds from a particular direction.

The bottom morphology of a lake can be greatly influenced by deposition of sediment carried by inflowing rivers and streams. Although this process can be modified by wave and current action, most lakes are sufficiently quiet to permit the formation of substantial deltas. In very old lake basins the relief may become so extensively decreased due to the great buildup of deltaic deposits and the long-term effects of river widening, that deposition on the outer portions of a delta will fail to balance the effects of wave erosion. A delta, in these circumstances, will begin to shrink in size.

It is very important to understand lake processes that affect the basin morphology and to be able to predict their trends and their impact on human activities. Increasingly, man is imposing his ability to change natural events in lakes, and he has often encountered problems by not anticipating a lake's reaction to his projects. The actual creation of a lake by damming a river is a major undertaking of this type. One fairly recent example is Lake Diefenbaker, in Saskatchewan. In this region of prairie farmland, the banks of the new lake are extremely vulnerable to erosion, and planners have had to contend with the consequences of bank cutting and infilling of the basin. There are many examples of lesser engineering undertakings that have had to face the consequences of a lake's reaction. The building of jetties or breakwaters, for example, may interfere with natural circulation features. In some cases this has resulted in the reduction of flow past a harbour and increase in flow past a previously stable shoreline, with the result that the harbour has filled in or been blocked by sediment deposition, while the stable shoreline has become badly eroded.

THE HYDROLOGIC BALANCE OF THE LAKES

The role of lakes within the global hydrologic cycle has been described earlier. Lakes depend for their very existence upon a balance between their many sources of water and the losses that they experience. This so-called water budget of lakes is important enough to have warranted considerable study throughout the world, with each lake or lake system possessing its own hydrologic idiosyncrasies. Aside from being of scientific interest, water-budget studies serve to reveal the dependence of each lake on particular hydrologic factors, thus enabling better management practices. These may include restrictions on water utilization during drought conditions, dike construction and evacuations prior to flooding, control of water levels to ensure efficient power production, and major decisions associated with diversions of watercourses in order to enhance water-quantity- and water-quality-management activities.

The net water balance for a particular lake will vary according to the periodic and nonperiodic variations of the inputs and outputs and is reflected in the fluctuations of the lake level. Because the prime influencing factors are meteorological, the periodicity of seasonal events are often seen in water-level records.

Ultimately, a lake will decline as a result of water loss or sediment infill. Over time, a number of biological, physical, and chemical factors work together to transform the lake and its basin into another physical entity.

THE WATER BUDGET

While people may accommodate to predicted imbalances in the hydrologic budget, it is usually difficult to influence the basic natural factors that cause the imbalances. Precipitation and evaporation, for the most part, are uncontrollable, although some advances have been made in evaporation suppression from small lakes through the use of monomolecular surface films. Groundwater flow is not controllable, except where highly restricted flow can be tapped. Rivers and streams, however, can be subjected to regulation by well-established practices through the use of dams, storage reservoirs, and diversions. It is mainly through these controls that efforts are made to make the most efficient usage of water as a resource.

When engineers take steps to alter elements of a basin's water budget, careful consideration must be given to the consequences of the hydrology and ecology of the entire watershed. Dredging operations for the purpose of harbour clearance or improvements to a navigable channel, for example, may increase the outflow from an upstream lake, increase shore erosion, or regenerate undesirable sedimentary constituents into the lake or river water. The damming of a river or a lake outlet to increase local water storage may also result in undesirable effects, such as an increased evaporation from the larger surface

Workers operating a dredger on a lake created for boating in Havasu City, Ariz. (U.S.). Photoshot/Hulton Archive/Getty Images

area, the restriction of fish movement, or changes in the thermal climate of the downstream flow. Diversions and dam-site construction may also result in flooding of important bird-breeding areas or a lowering of other lakes in the system, resulting in undesirable consequences.

WATER INPUT

The usual major input of water to a lake derives from streams and rivers, precipitation, and groundwater. In some cases inflow may come directly from glacier melt. The relative importance of each of the major sources varies from lake to lake.

Stream and river flow are usually seasonally variable, depending upon precipitation cycles and snowmelt. At low altitudes some rivers exhibit a peak during a high precipitation period in winter and then a second peak associated with a subsequent spring snowmelt that feeds the nearby high-altitude tributaries. In regions where precipitation can occur in great quantities at high rates, streams swell quickly and water is delivered in relatively large volumes to downstream lakes.

A great deal of work has been done to improve the ability to measure and record streamflow. Consequently, it is usually the most accurately known of the inflow terms in the water budget. Most frequently, the height of the river level (stage) correlates well with the water discharge. In other cases, direct river-flow measurements are taken periodically with flow meters.

Precipitation reaching a lake's surface directly may be the major input. This is true of Lake Victoria, in eastern Africa. In other cases, where the lake basin is large with well-developed drainage to a deep lake of small surface area, precipitation may be a small component. Precipitation that falls elsewhere in the lake basin may reach the lake through either surface or groundwater flow, or it may be lost due to evapotranspiration.

Measurements or estimates of precipitation for a basin are difficult to achieve. Even where elaborate networks of rain gauges exist or where these are supplemented by meteorological radar installations, total basin-precipitation data are still considered to be poor. Measurements of direct precipitation over lakes are exceedingly rare. This situation is especially serious in the case of a large lake for which nearby land data are not necessarily representative of conditions over the lake. Each climatic region throughout the world has its typical precipitation pattern, and the lakes within the regions are affected accordingly.

Groundwater reaches lakes either through general seepage or through fissures (springs). Groundwater is taken to be water in that zone of saturation that has as its surface the water table. The depth of the water table can be determined by digging a well into the saturated zone and noting the level of water—unless the water is under pressure, in which case it will rise in the well to a level above the water table. Clearly, it is possible for a lake level to coincide with the water table. In fact, unless impermeable material intervenes, the water table will drop to, rise to, or lie level with a lake surface. Groundwater that is lost from the saturated zone to a lake is termed groundwater discharge. Groundwater introduced to the saturated zone from a lake is termed recharge. The rate at which groundwater is exchanged between a lake and the saturated zone depends mainly upon the level of the water table and the pressure conditions within the saturated zone.

In permeable materials the zone above the water table is called the zone of aeration, and water within it is called soil moisture. Soil moisture is classified into three types: hygroscopic water adsorbed on the surface of soil particles, water held by surface tension in capillary spaces in the soil and moving in response to capillary forces, and water that drains through the soil under gravitational influence. The latter will most significantly contribute to groundwater recharge and to the water balance of a lake. The second category will generally be subject to loss due to transpiration by plants.

WATER OUTPUT

Lakes that have no outlets, either above or below surface, are termed closed lakes, whereas those from which water is lost through surface or groundwater flows are called open lakes. Closed lakes, therefore, lose water only through evaporation. In these cases, the loss of water that is less saline than the source water results in an increasing lake salinity.

Evaporation results from a vertical gradient of vapour pressure over the water surface. Next to the water surface, saturation conditions exist that are a function of the temperature at the interface. The vapour pressure in the air above the surface is calculated from the temperature of the air and the wet-bulb temperature. The rate at which evaporation occurs also depends upon the factors that affect the removal of the saturated air above the surface, such as wind speed and thermal convection.

Studies of evaporation must surely constitute a sizable proportion of all hydrological and oceanographic work. The principal categories of evaporation studies are water budget, energy budget, bulk aerodynamic techniques, and direct measurements of vapour flux.

The so-called aerodynamic technique is based upon Dalton's formula, which correlates evaporation with the product of the vapour pressure gradient and the wind speed. Studies during the past 20 years have produced a host of variations of this equation, determined empirically using independent measurements of evaporation. One of the most often used of these was developed in a study of Lake Hefner, and even this work has been subsequently modified to suit other climates and conditions. Few workers are satisfied with the present state of the art in the use of the aerodynamic equations. Nevertheless, once an equation of this type is satisfactorily developed for a particular lake, having been checked with independent methods, it is attractive because it usually employs data that can be routinely observed.

The direct measurement of vapour fluxes is an extremely intricate proposition, as motions over a water surface are usually turbulent, and instruments capable of measuring rapidly changing vertical motions and humidities are required. Not the least of the difficulties is the likelihood that the kind of turbulence over large bodies far from land is significantly different from that over land.

Evaporation pans attempt to simulate, but cannot completely duplicate, the climactic conditions on a lake. They do, however, help scientists estimate the rate of lake-water evaporation. NOAA/National Weather Service/North Indiana Weather Forecast Office

Recent advances in theoretical developments and instrumentation continue to encourage this type of study. In turn, successes in this field offer the opportunity for the refinement of empirical techniques more practically suited for general lake investigators.

In many lake studies, data from evaporation pans have been used to determine lake evaporation. Pans have even been developed for flotation on lakes. Pans cannot truly simulate lakes, however, as they constitute a different type of system (they are not exposed to the atmosphere in the same way, they exchange heat through their sides, and they do not store heat in the same way as lakes).

Some examples of evaporation estimates include annual totals of between 60 and 90 cm (two and three feet) for Lake Ontario (using different techniques and for different years); about 75 cm (2.5 feet) for Lake

Mendota, Wisconsin; over 210 cm (seven feet) for Lake Mead, Arizona and Nevada; about 140 cm (4.5 feet) for Lake Hefner; about 660 mm (26 inches) for the IJsselmeer, in the Netherlands; and about 109 mm (4.25 inches) for Lake Baikal.

Water output from a lake in the form of surface-water outflow generally depends upon the lake level and the capacity of the effluent channel. Although lakes often have many surface inflows or at least several incoming streams or rivers, they generally have but one surface effluent.

WATER-LEVEL FLUCTUATIONS

Lake-level rises generally coincide with or closely follow seasons of high precipitation, and falls of level generally coincide with seasons of high evaporation. Complications are introduced by a variety of factors, however. The storage of heavy winter precipitation as snowpack is one example. The release of this water during the spring thaw may also be hampered by the presence of river ice, resulting in late-spring or summer peaks. In large drainage basins the full effects of heavy precipitation may not be immediately realized in the lake-water balance because of the time required for basin drainage. Where glacier melt is a major input to a lake, the changes in level respond to seasonal heating as well as seasonal precipitation.

Although artificial controls, in the form of diversions, river dredging, and dams, affect the levels of the Great Lakes, the latter provide good examples of seasonal variations because of the lengthy record of levels available. The rivers draining to these large lakes are relatively stable; that is, the ratio of maximum to minimum flow is about 2 or 3 to 1, compared to 30 to 1 for the Mississippi River and 35 to 1 for the Columbia River. A 67-year average of lake

An Aymara Indian poling a reed boat on Lake Titicaca, near the Bolivian shore. Titicaca's water level fluctuates seasonally and over a cycle of years. © Tony Morrison/South American Pictures

levels by month shows that high water occurs, on the average, in September for Lake Superior and in June for Lake Ontario. Lows occur in March and December–January, respectively. The mean range in seasonal levels, for this period, is about 30 cm (1 foot) for Lake Superior and about 45 cm (1.5 feet) for Lake Ontario. The pattern varies considerably from year to year, however, and periods of exceptional precipitation and drought are shown in the records. These events ultimately affect the downstream lakes, but, because of their relatively small discharge volumes, it takes 3.5 years for 60 percent of the full effect of a supply change to Lake Huron–Michigan to appear in the outflow from Lake Ontario.

The seasonal changes in a lake's level may be superimposed on longer-term trends, which in some cases dominate. Several of the large lakes of the world have water-level records that illustrate long-term periods of relative abundance of water and drought. In Central Africa, Lakes Victoria, Albert, Tanganyika, and Nyasa exhibit substantial long-term features, some of which are consistent, suggesting that a common climatological factor is responsible. Nevertheless, others of these features are not consistent within the lakes and have not been adequately explained.

The principal climatological factors that would most affect long-term lake-level variations have not been recorded for long periods at many locations. Regular precipitation observations were not made before about 1850. Some useful evidence is found in such natural records as tree rings and peat-bog stratigraphy.

On a worldwide basis, there is evidence of a period of low levels in the middle 19th century and near the end of the first quarter of the 20th century. Lake George, in Australia, the Caspian Sea, several lakes in western North America, and Pangong Lake, in Tibet, are examples that have exhibited these features.

LAKE EXTINCTION

The life history of a lake may take place over just a few days, in the case of one formed by a beaver dam, or, for the largest lakes, it may cover geologic time periods. A lake may come to its end physically through loss of its water or through infilling by sediments and other materials. Reference has previously been made to the chemical-biological death of a lake, which is not necessarily the end of it as a physical entity but may in fact be its termination as a desirable body of water.

Geologic processes involving the uplift and subsequent erosion of mountains and the advance and retreat of glaciers establish lake basins and then proceed to destroy them through infilling. Lake basins may also lose their water through drought or through changes in the drainage pattern that result in depletion of water inflows or enhancement of outflows.

The chemical-biological changes within a lake's history offer a fine example of ecological succession. In the early stages a lake contains little organic material and has a poorly developed littoral zone. Particularly in temperate zones, such conditions favour a plentiful oxygen content, and the lake is said to be oligotrophic. As erosion progresses and as lake enrichment and organic content increase, the lake may become sufficiently productive to place an excessive demand upon the oxygen content. When periods of oxygen depletion occur, a lake is said to be eutrophic. An intermediate stage in this course of events is called mesotrophy. In the case of oligotrophy the vertical oxygen distribution is essentially uniform, or orthograde. Under eutrophic conditions, oxygen values decrease with depth, and the vertical distribution is called clinograde.

The limits of oligotrophic and eutrophic conditions have been set in terms of the rate at which oxygen is depleted from the hypolimnion. These limits are arbitrary but are approximately 0.03 and 0.05 milligrams per square centimetre per day as the upper limit of oligotrophy and the lower limit of eutrophy, respectively.

As eutrophic conditions develop, bottom sediments become enriched in organic material, and bottom plants spread throughout the littoral zone. As infilling proceeds, the plant-choked littoral zone spreads lakeward. Eventually, the littoral zone becomes a marsh, and the central part of the lake diminishes to a pond. When the lake finally ceases to exist, terrestrial vegetation may flourish, even to the extent of forestation.

CHAPTER 3
INLAND WATER ECOSYSTEMS

An inland water ecosystem is a complex of living organisms in free water on continental landmasses. Inland waters represent parts of the biosphere within which marked biological diversity, complex biogeochemical pathways, and an array of energetic processes occur. Although from a geographic perspective inland waters represent only a small fraction of the biosphere, when appreciated from an ecological viewpoint, they are seen to be major contributors to biospheric diversity, structure, and function.

THE ORIGIN OF INLAND WATERS

Only a relatively small fraction of the total amount of water in the biosphere is found as free water on continental landmasses. The oceans contain about 97.6 percent of the biosphere's water, and polar ice, groundwater, and water vapour take up another 2.4 percent. Thus, less than 1 percent exists as continental free water, which is generally referred to as inland water. In spite of this small percentage, inland water is an essential element of the biosphere. It occurs in a wide variety of forms and is inhabited by a diverse set of biological communities, quite distinct from the communities of marine and terrestrial ecosystems.

All inland waters originate from the ocean, principally through evaporation, and ultimately return to this source. This process is part of the global hydrologic cycle. A major feature of this cycle is that more water evaporates from the ocean than is directly precipitated back into it. The balance of water vapour is precipitated as rain, snow, or hail over continental landmasses whence it either evaporates into the atmosphere (about 70 percent) or drains into the sea.

On the surface of the land, free water habitats can be classified as either lotic (running-water) or lentic (standing-water). Lotic habitats include rivers, streams, and brooks, and lentic habitats include lakes, ponds, and marshes. Both habitats are linked into drainage systems of three major sorts: exorheic, endorheic, and arheic. Exorheic regions are open systems in which surface waters ultimately drain to the ocean in well-defined patterns that involve streams and rivers temporarily impounded by permanent freshwater lakes. Endorheic regions are considered closed systems because, rather than draining to the sea, surface waters drain to inland termini, whence they evaporate or seep away. Typically, the termini are permanent or temporary lakes that become saline as evaporation concentrates dissolved salts that either have been introduced by rainwater or have been leached out of substrata within the drainage basin. In arheic systems water falls unpredictably in small amounts and follows haphazard drainage patterns. Apart from rivers that arise outside the region (allogenic rivers) and areas fed from underground sources of water, most bodies of water within arheic regions are temporary.

Inland water also is found beneath the land's surface. Considerable amounts of groundwater are found within permeable rock strata, and bodies of water are found within caves and other subterranean rock formations, generally of limestone. Subsurface inland waters also are important in the global hydrologic cycle, and some are of biological interest.

On the basis of whether inland waters are lotic or lentic, permanent or temporary, fresh or saline, it is possible to distinguish five major types of inland waters: among lentic systems are three types—permanent freshwater, temporary freshwater, and permanent saline—and among lotic systems are two types—permanent and temporary. These types are not equally distributed among the continents. As one would expect, permanent waters, both lotic and lentic, are more characteristic of temperate and tropical regions, and temporary waters, again both lotic and lentic, are found more often in dry regions. Salt lakes are also more characteristic of dry regions. Whatever the major type of water, however, drainage lines and basins are necessary for inland waters to occur. These features result from many geologic processes, such as erosion and sedimentation. Lentic waters occupy basins formed by glaciers, volcanoes, rivers, wind, tectonics (movements of the Earth's crust), and chemical weathering. Humans also have created many lakelike habitats, including reservoirs, impoundments, and farm dams. Lotic waters develop in the lowest topographic area of the landscape, which is eroded and sculpted by water flowing through it.

PERMANENT BODIES OF STANDING FRESH WATER

About half of all inland waters reside in deep, permanent, freshwater lakes. The largest of these lakes is Lake Baikal in Russia, which contains almost 20 percent of the total amount of inland fresh water. Another 20 percent is found in the Great Lakes of North America. Characteristic of such waters is the development of vertical differences (vertical stratification) of several important features, which often display marked seasonal variation as well. Light is by far the most important variable feature because it supplies not only chemical energy for biological processes but also heat. It is the diurnal, seasonal, and vertical differences in heat that ultimately give rise to most other spatiotemporal, physicochemical differences within lakes.

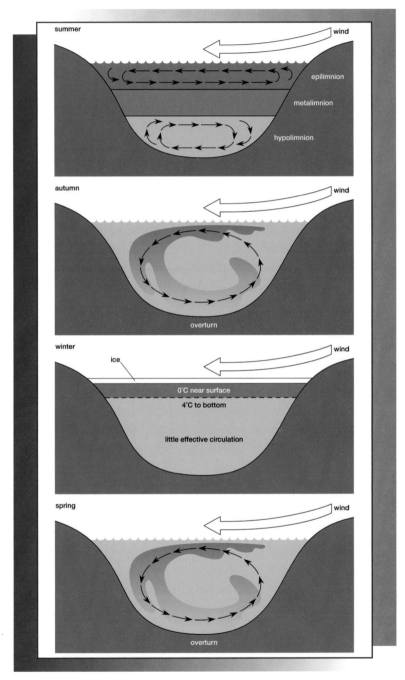

Annual circulation patterns in a dimictic lake. Encyclopædia Britannica, Inc.

Various thermal patterns typically occur in deep, freshwater lakes. In temperate regions of the biosphere, where a majority of such lakes occur, lakes exhibit a dimictic thermal pattern (two periods of mixing—in spring and autumn—per year) caused by seasonal differences in temperature and the mixing effects of wind. This type of lake stratifies in summer as the surface water (epilimnion) warms and ceases to mix with the lower, colder layer (hypolimnion). Water circulates within but not between the layers, more vigorously within the epilimnion. The boundary between these layers is the metalimnion, a zone of rapid temperature change. With the onset of autumn, the epilimnion cools and the water becomes denser, sinking and mixing with the hypolimnion.

The work required to mix the two layers is provided by wind, and the lake circulates, or overturns, completely. Circulation continues until surface ice protects the lake from further wind action. The lake overturns again in spring after surface ice melts, and by summer it will be stratified once again. Other thermal patterns are monomixis, in which a single annual period of circulation alternates with a single thermal stratification event, and polymixis, in which frequent periods of stratification occur.

During winter, surface ice prevents further mixing by the wind. Small differences in density and temperature exist, with cooler water (0°C) staying near the surface and warmer, more dense water (4°C) extending to the bottom.

Many other physicochemical features exhibit seasonal differences in vertical distribution. Most are closely associated with and dependent upon seasonal thermal differences. For example, in the summer the epilimnion of dimictic lakes may contain high concentrations of dissolved oxygen, and the hypolimnion low concentrations. The reverse may apply to dissolved carbon dioxide. Aside from the summer season, however, no vertical differences may be present. Changes in oxygen concentration are particularly important because many aquatic animals cannot survive when oxygen concentrations dip below a certain level. Oxygen concentrations also determine the solubility of several important substances, notably phosphate, iron, and manganese, which consequently display vertical seasonal variation as well.

Some features of deep, freshwater lakes, such as water level and salinity, do not vary seasonally. Neither does salinity have a vertical gradient within such lakes. Few physicochemical features of shallow, permanent bodies of

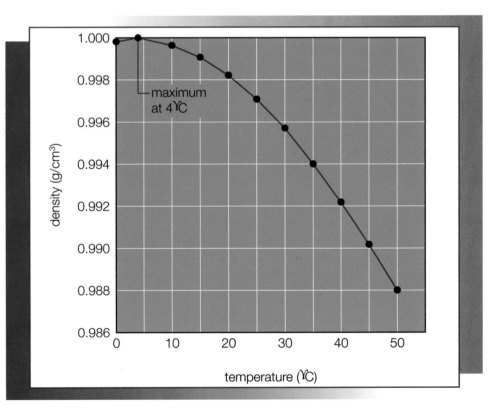

Relationship between the density of pure water and temperature. Encyclopædia Britannica, Inc.

standing fresh water are vertically stratified, although many features vary significantly according to season. However, in permanent bodies of fresh water located in regions warmer than the temperate zone, thermal stratification and related phenomena may develop at shallower depths and persist longer than they would in temperate lakes of similar morphometry. This follows from the water density–temperature relationship, according to which, at higher temperatures, water density changes rapidly with only small temperature rises.

TEMPORARY BODIES OF STANDING FRESH WATER

All land surfaces in the biosphere develop temporary bodies of fresh water following a rain. Although the total volume of fresh water in such localities is only a small fraction of that in permanent freshwater lakes, the biological role of temporary bodies of standing fresh water is considerable. They represent one of the most characteristic types of bodies of water in all arid landscapes of the biosphere (which make up about one-third of total land area). In certain regions and at particular times they represent the most obvious landscape feature (e.g., on the Highveld of South Africa). Many types occur, ranging from small, short-lived rainpools of irregular occurrence to large, regularly flooded wetlands that persist for many months. Because of their ubiquity, these temporary bodies of water are known by many names, including those of local derivation such as vlei, claypan, pan, playa, and tinaja. The length of time that temporary waters last and the timing and regularity of their occurrence depend primarily on climatic and topographic features. As a general rule, however, the more arid the environment, the shorter their life span and the less predictable their occurrence.

Temporary bodies of water are usually shallow; thus, vertical differences in physicochemical features are not as apparent in these waters as they are in permanent, deeper waters. When vertical differences do develop, they are generally transient (with the exception of thermal stratification in regions of high temperatures, as noted previously). Physicochemical features in temporary bodies of water are much more sensitive to external events than they are in deeper, permanent waters. Thus, hydrologic variability (e.g., inputs, water levels, depths), sediment-water interchange, and wind have greater effects than they do in deep, permanent, freshwater lakes. (Salinity, however, rarely fluctuates above 3 grams per litre.) Overall, it may be said that aquatic ecosystems in temporary bodies of standing fresh water are much less buffered from external environmental events than are permanent bodies of fresh water.

SALINE LAKES

Saline lakes (i.e., bodies of water that have salinities in excess of 3 grams per litre) are widespread and occur on all continents, including Antarctica. Saline lakes include the largest lake in the world, the Caspian Sea; the lowest lake, the Dead Sea; and many of the highest lakes, such as those in Tibet and on the Altiplano of South America. Although inland saline water constitutes some 45 percent of total inland water, it is largely concentrated in only a few deep lakes, principally the Caspian Sea. Saline lakes are most common in the semiarid regions of the biosphere, which encompass approximately 27 percent of total land area, because two preconditions for the formation of salt lakes occur there most frequently: a balance between input of water (precipitation and inflows) and output of water (evaporation and seepage) and the presence of endorheic drainage basins.

Despite their wide geographic distribution and large total volume, the importance of salt lakes as an integral element in biospheric processes generally has been overlooked. Indeed, not until the effects of human impact began to be noticed—from about 1960—did their environmental significance become clear. An example of this is provided by the Aral Sea, a large salt lake in Central Asia. After much of the input of fresh water was diverted before reaching the lake to be used for irrigation, the level of the lake fell, salinity rose, and vast expanses of the lake bed were exposed. As a result, the fishing industry collapsed, islands that had served as wildlife refuges became peninsulas, biological diversity and productivity fell, biota disappeared, large quantities of salt blew from the lake bed onto neighbouring lands, groundwater salinity rose, and the local climate was altered. The effects on the local human population were catastrophic as well.

Permanent salt lakes show the same sort of vertical differences in physicochemical attributes as permanent bodies of standing fresh water do; similarly, temporary salt lakes and temporary bodies of standing fresh water respond alike to environmental disturbances. However, all salt lakes are distinguished from all freshwater bodies by differences in ionic composition and, obviously, much higher salinities. Depending on the dominant ions present, salinities may reach values well above 300 grams per litre. In permanent, deep salt lakes, annual salinities as well as water levels may fluctuate only slightly, while, in shallow, temporary lakes, salinities may range from less than 50 grams per litre to more than 300 grams per litre over a period of a single year and be accompanied by wide water-level fluctuations. Moreover, because all salt lakes are dependent on a climatic balance, they are a great deal more sensitive to long-term climatic changes than are freshwater lakes. Thus, even large, deep, permanent salt lakes display marked changes in salinity and water level over time, reflecting long-term shifts in climate. Often these changes are compounded by the human diversion of water, as described above. Salinity has many direct effects on other physicochemical features. Its effect on freezing points has already been noted. Salinity also affects the amount of oxygen that can be dissolved. The greater the concentration of sodium chloride, which is the solution most similar to that encountered in saline lakes, the less soluble is oxygen.

THE BIOTA OF INLAND WATERS

A remarkably diverse assemblage of plants, animals, and microbes live in inland waters, with nearly all major groups of living organisms found in one sort of aquatic ecosystem or another. Nevertheless, no major group actually evolved in inland waters; all evolved either in the sea or on land, whence the biological invasion of inland waters eventually took place. The long period of time since this original invasion occurred, however, has allowed many important taxa of inland waters, such as different types of crustaceans, to evolve.

The only major groups of aquatic animals conspicuously absent from inland waters include the phyla Echinodermata, Ctenophora, and Hemichordata. Several other major groups of aquatic animals, as well as plants, are markedly less diverse in inland waters than they are in the sea: Notable among the animals are the phyla Porifera (sponges), Cnidaria, and Bryozoa (moss animals) and among the plants are Phaeophyta (brown algae) and Rhodophyta (red algae). The reason these groups did not invade as successfully as other groups is uncertain, but presumably they were less able to cope with lower salinities and reduced environmental stability. Major groups of the inland aquatic biota that are derived from terrestrial ancestors are insects and macrophytes other than large algae.

Whatever their origins, the invading biota needed to develop many adaptations to the special physicochemical features of inland waters. For those abandoning a marine environment the primary adaptation was a physiologic one that would permit survival in a considerably less saline, more dilute external medium. For terrestrial biota, the most necessary adaptations were those that would allow the organism to exist in a medium of significantly greater density and viscosity that also contained less oxygen. Many other adaptations were required to meet the challenges that particular features of a given aquatic environment posed. Thus, in running waters adaptations were needed that prevented an organism from being washed downstream; in highly saline lakes, a concentrated external medium was the challenging environmental feature; and in temporary waters, the main obstacle was to survive the dry phase. The adaptations themselves are many and varied and include those of physiology (e.g., osmoregulatory abilities), structure (e.g., flattened bodies of fauna living in running waters), behaviour (e.g., burrowing to avoid dehydration), and ecology (e.g., development of life cycles that accord with the occurrence of seasonally unfavourable conditions).

The biota of almost all inland saline waters did not evolve directly from marine ancestors but instead primarily from freshwater forms. Only a few forms appear to be of terrestrial derivation, and a few organisms in inland waters located near coasts are of marine origin. Although at first this evolutionary pathway may not seem obvious, it can be explained easily. Organisms that survive under greater environmental stress tend to have a greater ability to adapt than those that do not. Marine environments are considered less stressful than freshwater environments; hence, organisms from fresh waters are better able to adapt to the extremely stressful environment of inland saline waters.

THE STRUCTURE OF INLAND WATER ECOSYSTEMS

All types of inland aquatic ecosystems have well-defined structures and processes that are similar in general aspects but differ in particular details throughout the biosphere. Thus, as is true of marine and terrestrial ecosystems, almost all inland aquatic ecosystems have three fundamental trophic levels—primary producers (algae and macrophytes), consumers (animals), and decomposers (bacteria, fungi, small invertebrates)—that are interconnected by a complex web of links. Energy passes through these trophic levels primarily along the grazer and detrital chains and is progressively degraded to heat through metabolic activities. Meanwhile, the essential elements follow pathways that cycle between these biotic components and the abiotic components of the ecosystem. A few inland aquatic ecosystems such as hot springs and highly saline lakes have conditions so inimical to life that biological diversity is restricted, trophic levels are correspondingly simple, and energetic and biogeochemical processes are compressed.

Organisms within the trophic network are arranged into populations and communities. In deep, freshwater lakes the primary producers (plants) are found either at the shallow edges of the lake (emergent, submerged, or floating macrophytes) or free-floating within its upper layers (microscopic algae, cyanobacteria, and photosynthetic bacteria of the plankton community). Plants are found only in the photic zone—the upper portion of the lake

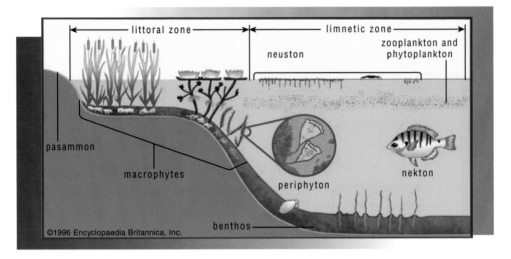

Major biological communities of freshwater lakes. Copyright Encyclopædia Britannica; rendering for this edition by Rosen Educational Services

where photosynthesis occurs, also called the trophogenic zone. In this zone the production of biochemical energy through photosynthesis is greater than its consumption through respiration and decomposition. Animals and decomposers are found in both the photic and aphotic zones. In the aphotic zone, also called the tropholytic zone, the consumption of energy exceeds its production. The zones are demarcated by a plane of compensation at which primary production and consumption are equivalent. This plane varies diurnally and seasonally with changes in light penetration. The major biological communities of deep freshwater lakes are made up of plankton, which contains tiny floating plants (phytoplankton) and animals (zooplankton) as well as microbes; the shoreline macrophytes; the benthos (bottom-dwelling organisms); the nekton (free-swimming forms in the water column); the periphyton (microscopic biota on submerged objects); the psammon (biota buried in sediments); and the neuston (biota associated with surface film). These organisms differ enormously in size, ranging from less than 0.5

micrometre (0.00002 inch) to greater than 1 metre (3.28 feet). They also vary in composition, structure, function, adaptations, and spatiotemporal location. Significant taxonomic differences also occur across continents; for example, the fish species of freshwater lakes in Africa are not the same as those of similar ecosystems in North America, nor are the plankton of lakes in Australia the same as those of lakes in Asia.

The populations and communities of inland waters other than freshwater lakes are similarly complex but markedly different in all except their fundamental ecological roles. Even major ecological and biogeochemical processes are quite distinct in different sorts of inland waters. In streams, for example, plankton populations are absent and much energy is derived allochthonously (from outside the stream). The processing and transport of essential elements follow a downstream sequence. Hypotheses attempting to explain ecological processes in running waters include the concept of the river continuum, which explains differences in lotic communities according to the changing ecological factors along the river system. Nutrient spiraling is another concept invoked to explain the cycling of nutrients while they are carried downstream. For large rivers of variable hydrology, the flood pulse concept has been instructive. This concept regards seasonal or occasional flood events as important ecological phenomena determining the biology of the river.

THE BIOLOGICAL PRODUCTIVITY OF INLAND WATER ECOSYSTEMS

Central to all biological activity within inland aquatic ecosystems is biological productivity or aquatic production. This involves two main processes: (1) primary production, in which living organisms form energy-rich organic material (biomass) from energy-poor inorganic materials in the environment through photosynthesis, and (2) secondary production, the transformation, through consumption, of this biomass into other forms. In this context, it is important to distinguish between gross primary production—i.e., the total amount of energy fixed by photosynthesis—and net primary production—i.e., the amount of energy fixed less that respired by the plants involved and available for secondary production. Note that forms of production using energy other than radiant energy from the Sun are not important to overall aquatic production.

Rates of production, factors that limit production, and the results of production have been and are matters of constant and fundamental interest in inland waters, not least because of the impact that different levels of production in certain waters have on human populations. Decreased levels of secondary production (e.g., a reduction in the fish population) can lead to a meagre harvest, which can in turn provide insufficient protein for some local human populations. Elevated levels of primary production brought about by the input of excess plant nutrients, principally phosphates and nitrates, into inland waters following agricultural and urban development of catchments (known as eutrophication), can also be harmful. For example, eutrophication often results in the development of algal blooms—i.e., dense populations of algae and cyanobacteria, which may be unsightly, toxic, malodorous, or otherwise harmful and unwanted.

Standing bodies of fresh water are often divided into categories that reflect levels of biological production. Oligotrophic lakes are those that are unproductive: net primary production is only between 50 and 100 milligrams of carbon per square metre per day, nutrients are in poor supply, and secondary production is depressed. Eutrophic lakes, on the other hand, are productive: net primary production is between 600 and 8,000 milligrams of carbon per square metre per day, nutrients are in good supply, and secondary production is high. Mesotrophic lakes are lakes of intermediate productivity: net primary production is between 250 and 1,000 milligrams of carbon per square metre per day. Models that relate levels of lake productivity to levels of nutrient input or loading have been useful in controlling eutrophication in many temperate freshwater lakes. It was once thought that lakes evolved from states of oligotrophy to eutrophy, but this is now generally believed not to be the case. Instead, lake productivity reflects contemporary processes of nutrient supply more than historical events.

As for comparative levels of biological productivity in inland waters, most values stand somewhere between the high values of coral reefs and the low values of deserts. It is difficult to generalize in this matter, however, because wide ranges in net primary production occur in any type of inland aquatic ecosystem. Certain communities, such as reedswamps in tropical lakes, have values for primary production that are among the highest of those recorded anywhere in the biosphere. Notwithstanding these high values, biological production in inland waters does not significantly contribute to biospheric production. Nevertheless, the use of inland waters by humans to enhance either terrestrial primary production (by irrigating crops) or secondary production on land (by supplying drinking water to stock) is a significant indirect contribution.

From space, Earth's major lakes are recognizable features, visible as large areas of blue surrounded on all sides by land. The largest lakes are found in the Northern Hemisphere, especially in Asia (which contains the Caspian Sea, Lake Baikal, Lake Balkhash, and others) and North America (which contains the Great Lakes, Lake Winnipeg, and others). The rift valley of eastern Africa also possesses several major inland water bodies.

DEAD SEA

The Dead Sea (Arabic: Al-Baḥr al-Mayyit; Hebrew: Yam HaMelaẖ), which is also known as Salt Sea, is a landlocked salt lake between Israel and Jordan. It lies some 400 metres (1,300 feet) below sea level—the lowest elevation and the lowest body of water on the surface of the Earth. Its eastern shore belongs to Jordan, and the southern half of its western shore belongs to Israel. The northern half of the western shore lies within the Palestinian West Bank and has been under Israeli occupation since the 1967 Arab-Israeli war.

The Dead Sea lies between the hills of Judaea to the west and the Transjordanian plateaus to the east. The Jordan River flows from the north into the Dead Sea, which is 80 km (50 miles) long and attains a width of 18 km (11 miles). Its surface area is about 1,020 square km (394 square miles). The peninsula of Al-Lisān (Arabic: "The Tongue") divides the lake on its eastern side into two unequal basins: the northern basin encompasses about three-fourths of the lake's total surface area and reaches a depth of 400 metres (1,300 feet); the southern basin is smaller and shallower (less than 3 metres [10 feet] on average). During biblical times and up to the 8th century CE, only the area around the northern basin was inhabited, and the lake was about 35 metres (115 feet) below its level of the late 20th century. It rose to its highest level (389 metres [1,275 feet] below sea level) in 1896 but receded again after 1935.

The name Dead Sea can be traced back at least to the Hellenistic epoch (323 to 30 BCE). The Dead Sea figures in biblical accounts dating to the time of Abraham (progenitor of the Hebrews) and the destruction of Sodom and Gomorrah (the two cities along the lake, according to the Hebrew bible, that were destroyed by fire from heaven because of their wickedness). The desolate wilderness beside the lake offered refuge to David (king of Israel) and later to Herod I (the Great; king of Judaea), who at the time of the siege of Jerusalem by the Parthians in 40 BCE barricaded himself in a fortress at Masada. Masada was the scene of a two-year siege that culminated in the mass suicide of its Jewish Zealot defenders and the occupation of the fortress by the Romans in 73 CE. The Jewish sect that left the biblical manuscripts known as the Dead Sea Scrolls took shelter in caves northwest of the lake.

The Dead Sea occupies part of a graben (a downfaulted block of the Earth's crust) between transform faults along a tectonic plate boundary that runs from the Red Sea–Gulf of Suez spreading centre to a convergent plate boundary in the Taurus Mountains. The eastern fault, along the edge of the Moab Plateau, is more readily visible from the lake than is the western fault, which marks the gentler Judaean upfold.

In the Jurassic and Cretaceous periods (about 200 to 65 million years ago), before the creation of the graben, an extended Mediterranean Sea covered Syria and Palestine. During the Miocene Epoch (23 to 5.3 million years ago), as the Arabian tectonic plate collided with the Eurasian plate to the north, upheaval of the seabed produced the upfolded structures of the Transjordanian highlands and the central range of Palestine, causing the fractures that allowed the Dead Sea graben to drop. At that time, the Dead Sea was probably about the size that it is today. During the Pleistocene Epoch (2,600,000 to 11,700 years ago), it rose to an elevation of about 200 metres (700 feet) above its modern level, forming a vast inland sea that stretched some 320 km (200 miles) from the Ḥula Valley area in the north to 64 km (40 miles) beyond its present southern limits. The Dead Sea did not spill over into the Gulf of Aqaba because it was blocked by a 30-metre (100-foot) rise in the highest part of Wadi Al-ʿArabah, a seasonal watercourse that flows in a valley to the east of the central Negev highlands.

Beginning about 2.5 million years ago, heavy stream-flow into the lake deposited thick sediments of shale, clay, sandstone, rock salt, and gypsum. Later, strata of clay, marl, soft chalk, and gypsum were dropped upon layers of sand and gravel. With the water evaporating faster than it was replenished by precipitation over the last 10,000 years, the lake gradually shrank to its present form. In so doing, it bared deposits that cover the Dead Sea valley to a thickness of about 2 to 6 km (1 to 4 miles).

The peninsula of Al-Lisān and Mount Sedom (historically Mount Sodom) resulted from movements of the Earth's crust. Mount Sedom's steep cliffs rise up from the south-western shore. Al-Lisān is formed of strata of clay, marl, soft chalk, and gypsum interbedded with sand and gravel. Both Al-Lisān and beds made of similar material on the western side of the Dead Sea valley dip to the east. It is assumed that the uplifting of Mount Sedom and Al-Lisān formed a southern escarpment for the Dead Sea. Later the sea broke through the western half of this escarpment to flood what is now the shallow southern end of the Dead Sea.

The Dead Sea lies in a desert. Rainfall is scanty and irregular. Al-Lisān averages about 65 mm (2.5 inches) of rain a year, the industrial site of Sedom (near historical Sodom) only about 50 mm (2 inches). Owing to the lake's low elevation and sheltered location, winter temperatures are mild, averaging 17 °C (63 °F) in January at the southern end at Sedom and 14 °C (58 °F) at the northern end; freezing temperatures are unheard of. Summer is very hot, averaging 34 °C (93 °F) in August at Sedom, with a recorded maximum of 51 °C (124 °F). Evaporation of the lake's waters—estimated at about 55 inches (1,400 mm) a year—often creates a thick mist above the lake. On the rivers the atmospheric humidity varies from 45 percent in May to 62 percent in October. Lake and land breezes, which are relatively common, blow off the lake in all directions in the daytime and then reverse direction to blow toward the centre of the lake at night.

The inflow from the Jordan River, whose high waters occur in winter and spring, averages 540 million cubic metres (19 billion cubic feet) per year. Four modest but perennial streams descend from Jordan on the east through deep gorges: the wadis Al-'Uẓaymī, Zarqā' Mā'īn, Al-Mawjib, and Al-Ḥasā. Down numerous other wadis, streams flow spasmodically and briefly from the neighbouring heights as well as from the depression of Wadi Al-'Arabah. Thermal sulfur springs also feed the rivers. Evaporation in summer and the intake of water, especially in winter and spring, cause seasonal variations in the level of the lake of from 30 to 60 cm (12 to 24 inches).

The waters of the Dead Sea are extremely saline, and the concentration of salt increases toward the bottom. In effect, two different masses of water exist in the lake. Down to a depth of 40 metres (130 feet), the temperature varies from 19 to 37 °C (66 to 98 °F), the salinity is slightly less than 300 parts per thousand, and the water is

Columns of salt rising from the extremely saline waters of the Dead Sea. Peter Carmichael/ASPECT

especially rich in sulfates and in bicarbonates. Beneath a zone of transition located between 40 and 100 metres (130 and 330 feet), the water has a uniform temperature of about 22 °C (72 °F) and a higher degree of salinity (approximately 332 parts per thousand); it contains hydrogen sulfide and strong concentrations of magnesium, potassium, chlorine, and bromine. The deep water is saturated with sodium chloride, which precipitates to the bottom. The deep water is fossilized (i.e., being very salty and dense, it remains permanently on the bottom); the near-surface water dates from a few centuries after biblical times.

The saline water has a high density that keeps bathers buoyant. The fresh water of the Jordan stays on the surface; in the spring its muddy colour can be traced across the lake as far as 50 km (30 miles) south of the point where the river empties into the Dead Sea.

The lake's extreme salinity excludes all forms of life except bacteria. Fish carried in by the Jordan or by smaller streams when in flood die quickly. Apart from the vegetation along the rivers, plant life along the shores is discontinuous and consists mainly of halophytes (plants that grow in salty or alkaline soil).

The Dead Sea constitutes an enormous salt reserve. Rock salt deposits also occur in Mount Sedom along the southwestern shore. The salt has been exploited on a small scale since antiquity. In 1929 a potash factory was opened near the mouth of the Jordan. Subsidiary installations were later built in the south at Sedom, but the original factory was destroyed during the 1948–49 Arab-Israeli war. A factory producing potash, magnesium, and calcium chloride was opened in Sedom in 1955. Another plant produces bromine and other chemical products.

Salt deposits on the southwestern shore of the Dead Sea near Masada, Israel. Z. Radovan, Jerusalem

Because of its location on the contested Jordanian-Israeli frontier, navigation on the Dead Sea is negligible. Its shores are nearly deserted, and permanent establishments are rare. Exceptions are the factory at Sedom, a few hotels and spas in the north, and, in the west, a kibbutz (an Israeli agricultural community) in the region of the 'En Gedi oasis. Small cultivated plots are also occasionally found on the lakeshore.

CASPIAN SEA

The Caspian Sea (Russian: Kaspiyskoye More; Persian: Darya-ye Khezer) is the world's largest inland body of water, lying to the east of the Caucasus Mountains and to the west of the vast steppe of Central Asia. Its name derives from the ancient Kaspi peoples, who once lived in Transcaucasia to the west; among its other historical names, Khazarsk and Khvalynsk derive from former peoples of the region, while Girkansk stems from Girkanos, "Country of the Wolves."

The elongated sea sprawls for nearly 1,200 km (750 miles) from north to south, although its average width is only 320 km (200 miles). It covers an area of about 386,400 square km (149,200 square miles)—larger than Japan—and its surface lies some 27 metres (90 feet) below sea level. The maximum depth, toward the south, is 1,025 metres (3,360 feet) below the sea's surface. The drainage basin of the sea covers some 3,625,000 square km (1,400,000 square miles). The sea contains some 78,200 cubic km (63.4 billion acre-feet or 18,800 cubic miles) of water—about one-third of the Earth's inland surface water. The sea is bordered in the northeast by Kazakhstan, in the southeast by Turkmenistan, in the south by Iran, in the southwest by Azerbaijan, and in the northwest by Russia.

The Caspian is the largest salt lake in the world, but this has not always been true. Scientific studies have shown that until geologically quite recent times, approximately 11 million years ago, it was linked, via the Sea of Azov, the Black Sea, and the Mediterranean Sea, to the world ocean. The Caspian is of exceptional scientific interest, because its history—particularly former fluctuations in both area and depth—offers clues to the complex geologic and climatic evolution of the region. Human-made changes, notably those resulting from the construction of dams, reservoirs, and canals on the immense Volga River system (which drains into the Caspian from the north), have affected the contemporary hydrologic balance. Caspian shipping and fisheries play an important role in the region's economy, as does the production of petroleum and natural gas in the Caspian basin. The sea's splendid sandy beaches also serve as health and recreation resorts.

PHYSICAL FEATURES

The Caspian basin, as a whole, is usually divided into the northern, middle, and southern Caspian, based partly on underwater relief and partly on hydrologic characteristics. The sea contains as many as 50 islands, mostly small. The largest are Chechen, Tyuleny, Morskoy, Kulaly, Zhiloy, and Ogurchin.

SHORELINE FEATURES

The shores of the northern Caspian are low and reflect the great accumulation of alluvial material washed down by the Ural, Terek, and, above all, Volga rivers, whose deltas are extensive. The western shore of the middle Caspian is hilly. The foothills of the Greater Caucasus Mountains loom close but are separated from the coast by a narrow marine plain. The Abşeron Peninsula, on which the city of Baku is sited, thrusts out into the sea there, while just to its south the floodplain of the Kura and Aras rivers forms the Kura-Aras Lowland along the western shore of the southern Caspian. The southwestern and southern Caspian shores are formed of the sediments of the Länkäran and Gīlän-Māzanderān lowlands, with the high peaks of the Talish and Elburz mountains rearing up close inland. The eastern shore of the southern Caspian is low, formed partly by sediments derived from the erosion of the cliffs along the sea. This shoreline is broken sharply by the low, hilly Cheleken and Türkmenbashi peninsulas. Just to the north, behind the east shore of the middle Caspian, is the Kara-Bogaz-Gol (Garabogazköl), formerly a shallow gulf of the Caspian but now a large lagoonlike embayment that is separated from the sea by a man-made embankment. For the most part, the eastern shore of the middle Caspian is precipitous, with the sea destroying the margin of the limestone plateaus of Tüpqaraghan and Kendyrli-Kayasansk.

The major rivers—the Volga, Ural, and Terek—empty into the northern Caspian, with their combined annual flow accounting for about 88 percent of all river water entering the sea. The Sulak, Samur, Kura, and a number of smaller rivers flow in on the western shore of the middle and southern Caspian, contributing about 7 percent of the total flow into the sea. The remainder comes in from the rivers of the southern, Iranian shore. Apart from the Atrak (Atrek) River of southern Turkmenistan, the sea's arid eastern shore is notable for a complete lack of permanent streams.

SUBMARINE FEATURES

The northern Caspian, with an area of 99,404 square km (38,380 square miles), is the shallowest portion of the sea, with an average depth of 4 to 8 metres (13 to 26 feet), reaching a maximum of 20 metres (66 feet) along the boundary with the middle Caspian. The bottom is formed of a monotonously rippling sedimentary plain, broken only by a line of southern bars and shoals—some of which provide foundations for Tyuleny and Kulaly islands and the Zhemchuzhny shoals—reflecting underlying structural rises. Beyond this belt, known as the Mangyshlak Bank, the middle Caspian, 137,917 square km (53,250 square miles) in area, forms an irregular depression with an abrupt western slope and a gentler eastern gradient. The shallowest portion—a shelf with depths reaching 100–140 metres (330–460 feet)—extends along both shores, with the western slope furrowed by submerged landslides and canyons. The remains of ancient river valleys have been discovered on the gentler eastern slope; the bottom of the depression comprises a plain that deepens to the west. The Abşeron Bank, a belt of shoals and islands rising from submerged elevations of older rocks, marks the transition to the southern Caspian, a depression covering about 149,106 square km (57,570 square miles). This depression is fringed by a shelf that is narrow to the west and south but widens to the east. A series of submerged ridges breaks up the relief to the north, but otherwise the bottom of the depression is a flat plain and contains the Caspian's greatest depths.

GEOLOGY

The relief of the Caspian Sea reflects its complex geologic structure. The northern Caspian Sea bottom is extremely old, dating to Precambrian times, or at least about 540 million years ago. The bottom of the northern and middle Caspian has a continental-type crustal structure. The northern portion is a section of the northern Caspian tectonic depression, a vast downwarp in the great ancient structural block known as the Russian Platform. The Mangyshlak Bank links the mountainous Tüpqaraghan Peninsula to the east with underlying western shore structures; these are the remnants of an outlying structural uplift of the Hercynian mountain-building movement, which occurred some 290 million years ago. It has been suggested that the middle Caspian depression resulted from a sagging at the edge of these ancient structures that occurred in late Paleozoic times, about 250 million years ago. The bottom of the middle Caspian is highly complex. To the west, the submarine shelf is part of the sagging edge of the Greater Caucasus Geosyncline, while the submerged Turan Platform in the east swells up in the feature known as the Kara-Bogaz (Garabogaz) Swell. The features of the Abşeron Peninsula region, along with the folded structures on the western side of the southern Caspian depression, derive from the Alpine mountain-building and folding processes (dating from some 26 to 10 million years ago) that created the Caucasus ranges. The border between the middle and southern Caspian is, in fact, still experiencing folding activity. The entire southern Caspian rests on a very ancient suboceanic-type basalt crustal structure, although this is covered in the south by huge accumulations of sedimentary layers many miles thick.

Until the beginning of the late Miocene Epoch (about 11 million years ago), the sea basin of the Caspian was connected to the Black Sea through the structural depression known as the Manych Trench (or Kuma-Manych Depression). After a late Miocene uplift, the Caspian became an enclosed body, with oceanic submarine characteristics preserved today only in the southern Caspian. The ocean connection was temporarily reestablished in the early Pleistocene Epoch (about 2.6 million years ago), and it is possible that there also was a link north across the Russian Plain to the Barents Sea of the Arctic Ocean.

Since about 2 million years ago, glaciers have advanced and retreated across the Russian Plain, and the Caspian Sea itself—in successive phases known as Baku, Khazar, and Khvalyn—alternately shrank and expanded. This process left a legacy in the form of peripheral terraces that mark old shorelines and can also be traced in the geologically recent underlying sedimentary layers.

The Caspian Sea bottom is now coated with recent sediments, finely grained in the shallow north but with shell deposits and oolitic sand—reflecting the high lime content of the Caspian waters—widespread in other coastal areas. Calcium carbonate also affects the composition of the much deeper bottom layers.

CLIMATE

The northern Caspian lies in a moderately continental climate zone, while the middle (and most of the southern) Caspian lies in the warm continental belt. The southwest is touched by subtropical influences, and this remarkable variety is completed by the desert climate prevailing on the eastern shore. Atmospheric circulation is dominated in winter by the cold, clear air of the Asiatic anticyclone, while in summer spurs of the Azores high-pressure and the South Asian low-pressure centres are influential. Complicating factors are the cyclonic disturbances rippling in from the west and the tendency of the Caucasus Mountains to block them. As a result of these factors, northerlies and northwesterlies (nearly one-third of occurrences) and southeasterlies (more than one-third) dominate circulation patterns. Savage storms are associated with northerly and southeasterly winds.

Summer air temperatures are fairly evenly distributed—average July to August figures range between 24 and 26 °C (75 and 79 °F), with a maximum of 44 °C (111 °F) on the sunbaked eastern shore—but winter monthly

average temperatures range from -10 °C (14 °F) in the
north to 10 °C (50 °F) in the south. Average annual rainfall,
falling mainly in winter and spring, varies from 8 to 67
inches (200 to 1,700 mm) over the sea, with the least falling in the east and the most in the southwestern region.
Evaporation from the sea surface is high, reaching 40
inches (1,015 mm) per year. Ice formation affects the
northern Caspian, which usually freezes completely by
January, and in very cold years ice that floats along the
western shore comes as far south as the Abşeron Peninsula.

HYDROLOGY

Short-term wind-induced fluctuations in the sea level can
measure up to 2 metres (7 feet), though their average is
about 60 cm (2 feet). Seiches (free or standing-wave oscillation of the sea surface mainly caused by winds and local
changes in atmospheric pressure) are typically less pro-
nounced. Tidal changes are but a few centimetres (or
inches), and seasonal rises induced by high spring water in
the rivers are not much greater.

One of the more fascinating aspects of study of the
Caspian has been the reconstruction of long-term fluctuations over the centuries from archaeological, geological,
and historical evidence. It seems that since the 1st century
BCE the Caspian's water level has fluctuated by at least 7
metres (23 feet). The main reasons for these long-term
fluctuations are climatic changes that determine a balance
between water gains (river influx and precipitation) and
losses (evaporation). During the first three decades of the
20th century, the level of the Caspian was close to 26
metres (86 feet) below sea level, but in 1977 it dropped to
29 metres (96 feet), the lowest level noted during the past
400 to 500 years. A rapid rise in water level began in
1978—in the mid-1990s the sea was at 26.5 metres (87 feet)
below sea level—but after 1995 the sea's level fell slightly.

The lowering that took place between 1929 and 1977 was attributed to climatic changes that increased evaporation and reduced river influx—amplified by reservoir construction on the Volga to supply river water for irrigation and industry. The rise in water level after 1978 also resulted from climate change causing an increase in the inflow from the Volga, which during some years was considerably greater than average. An increase in precipitation over the sea itself and decrease of evaporation also contributed to the phenomenon. In 1980 Soviet hydrologists stemmed the outflow into the Kara-Bogaz-Gol by constructing sand barricades between the Caspian and the lagoon. Planners have given serious attention to the feasibility of other measures for stabilizing the Caspian's water level.

In summer, the average surface temperature of the Caspian ranges from 24 to 26 °C (75 to 79 °F), with the south a little warmer. There are, however, significant winter contrasts, from 3 to 7 °C (37 to 45 °F) in the north to 8 to 10 °C (46 to 50 °F) in the south. Upwellings of deep water at the eastern shore—a result of prevailing-wind activity—can also bring a marked drop in summer temperature.

Salinity in the Caspian is about 12.8 parts per thousand on average, but this conceals a variation from a mere 1 part per thousand near the Volga outlet to a high of 200 parts per thousand in the Kara-Bogaz-Gol, where intense evaporation occurs. In the open sea, distribution of salinity is markedly uniform; from the surface to the bottom it increases by only 0.1 to 0.2 part per thousand. Caspian waters differ from those of the ocean in their high sulfate, calcium, and magnesium carbonate content and—as a result of river inflow—lower chloride content.

Circulation of water masses occurs, basically, in a counterclockwise movement (north-to-south along the western shore), with a complex pattern developing farther south, where there are several subsidiary movements. Currents can be speeded up where they coincide with strong winds, and the sea surface is often ruffled by wave action. The maximum storm waves, occurring near the Abşeron Peninsula, have been measured at more than 9 metres (30 feet).

MARINE LIFE

About 850 animal and more than 500 plant species live in the Caspian; although the number of species is relatively low for a body of water of this size, many of them are endemic (i.e., found only there). Blue-green algae (cyano-bacteria) and diatoms constitute the greatest biomass concentrations, and there are several species of red and brown algae. Animal life—which has been affected greatly by changes in salinity—includes such fish species as sturgeon, herring, pike, perch, and sprat; several species of mollusks; and a variety of other organisms including sponges. Some 15 species of Arctic (e.g., the Caspian seal) and Mediterranean types complement the basic fauna. Some organisms have migrated to the Caspian relatively recently: barnacles, crabs, and clams, for example, have been transported by sea vessels, while gray mullets have been deliberately introduced by humans.

STUDY AND EXPLORATION

The scientific exploration of the Caspian Sea began in the 18th century on the initiative of Peter I the Great. The first report on the sea was published by the Russian Academy of Sciences in 1720. A description of the sea by Fedor I. Soimonov, which contained the first navigational instructions, and an atlas of the sea were both published in 1731. Hydrographic exploration of the Caspian basin was continued by the Russian navy and was completed mainly in the second half of the 19th century. The important measurements of the sea's surface level were initiated at Baku in 1830 and are now conducted at more than 20 locations.

The first multidisciplinary investigations of the Caspian Sea (hydrologic, chemical, and biological) were conducted during the expeditions (1904, 1912–13, and 1914–15) led by the Russian zoologist Nikolai M. Knipovich. Regular hydrometeorological observations were started in the 1920s. Investigations of the sea are now coordinated by the Scientific Council of the Caspian Sea. The most important programs are those studying long-term fluctuations in the regime and water level of the sea, the protection of the marine environment, and the preservation of the sea's biological productivity and unique natural features. With the breakup of the Soviet Union and the development of political conflicts in the region, little major research was undertaken during the 1990s. However, toward the end of the decade scientific research began to address environmental problems in the region.

GREAT BEAR LAKE

Great Bear Lake is located in the northern Fort Smith region and southeastern Inuvik region, Northwest Territories, Canada, lying astride the Arctic Circle. It was discovered before 1800 by North West Company traders and later named for the bears that inhabited its shores.

Irregular in shape and containing many small islands, Great Bear Lake is roughly 320 km (200 miles) long and 40–175 km (25–110 miles) wide and has a maximum depth of 413 metres (1,356 feet). Its area of 31,328 square km (12,096 square miles) makes it the largest lake entirely within Canada and the fourth largest in North America. The lake's cold, clear waters abound with fish, notably the speckled trout. The localities of Echo and Sawmill bays on the eastern shore and the trading post of Fort Franklin on the west are the lake's main settlements. The 113-km- (70-mile-) long Great Bear River, which drains the lake westward through marshes into the Mackenzie River, forms an important transportation link during its four ice-free months.

THE GREAT LAKES

The Great Lakes are made up of a chain of deep freshwater lakes in east-central North America comprising Lakes Superior, Michigan, Huron, Erie, and Ontario. They are one of the great natural features of the continent and of the Earth. Although Lake Baikal in Russia has a larger volume of water, the combined area of the Great Lakes—some 244,106 square km (94,250 square miles)—represents the largest surface of fresh water in the world, covering an area exceeding that of the United Kingdom. Their drainage basin of 765,888 square km (about 295,710 square miles), which includes the areas of the lakes themselves and their connecting waterways, extends approximately 1,100 km (690 miles) from north to south and about 1,380 km (860 miles) from Lake Superior in the west to Lake Ontario in the east. Except for Lake Michigan, the lakes provide a natural border between Canada and the United States, a frontier that was stabilized by a boundary-waters treaty of 1909. It is a source of pride for both countries that there are no fortifications or warships along the boundary.

Individually, the lakes rank among the 14 largest in the world. They played a central role in the European colonization and development of North America and for decades have attracted people and industry; Lakes Erie and Ontario and the southern portion of Lake Michigan are now ringed with large population concentrations. The lakes have not benefited from this development, however, and have been seriously affected by pollution. Concern over the fate of the lakes reached a high pitch in the late 20th century, with both the U.S. and the Canadian governments and individuals investigating methods for reversing the consequences of years of misuse of the lakes' waters.

The Great Lakes form the western portion of the larger St. Lawrence hydrographic system. This system extends generally eastward from the St. Louis River in Minnesota (which flows into Lake Superior), through the lakes and the St. Lawrence River, and empties into the Atlantic Ocean at the Gulf of St. Lawrence.

LAKE ERIE

Lake Erie is the fourth largest of the five Great Lakes of North America. It forms the boundary between Canada (Ontario) to the north and the United States (Michigan, Ohio, Pennsylvania, and New York) to the west, south, and east. The major axis of the lake extends from west-southwest to east-northeast for 388 km (241 miles), and the lake has a maximum width of 92 km (57 miles). The total area of the lake's drainage basin is 78,062 square km (30,140 square miles), exclusive of surface area, which is 25,670 square km (9,910 square miles).

The lake's principal tributary rivers are the Detroit (carrying the discharge of Lake Huron), Huron, and Raisin rivers of Michigan; the Maumee, Portage, Sandusky, Cuyahoga, and Grand rivers of Ohio; the Cattaraugus Creek of New York; and the Grand River of Ontario. The lake discharges at its eastern end through the Niagara River, and its western end contains all of the islands, the largest being Pelee Island, Ont. With a mean surface height of 170 metres (570 feet) above sea level, Erie has the smallest mean depth (19 metres [62 feet]) of the Great Lakes, and its deepest point is 64 metres (210 feet).

Because of its small size and shallow character, the lake has a comparatively short water-retention time of 2.6 years. Storms frequently cause short-period fluctuations in lake level that can amount to several feet at the ends of the lake. It is an important link in the St. Lawrence Seaway. The New York State Barge Canal has an outlet at Tonawanda, N.Y., on the Niagara River, and one of its branches enters Lake Erie at Buffalo.

Originally, a few harbours on the lake were formed by natural bays, but most of them are at the mouths of streams that were improved by protective piers, jellies, and breakwaters and by dredging to accommodate the large lake vessels. The industrial economy of the lakeshore area depends heavily upon water transportation. The important steel industry (notably, to the south at Pittsburgh and at Detroit) depends upon the movement of iron ore and limestone across the Great Lakes to Lake Erie ports (mostly to the Ohio ports of Cleveland, Ashtabula, and Conneaut). The port at Toledo, Ohio, handles soft-coal shipments, and Buffalo is an important grain port. Other prominent ports are Sandusky, Huron, Lorain, and Fairport Harbor (in Ohio), Erie (in Pennsylvania), and Port Colborne (in Ontario). Intense pollution of the lake resulted in the closing of many beaches and resorts in the 1960s, but by the late 1970s the environmental damage had begun to be arrested. Point Pelee National Park lies on the northwestern shore in southern Ontario.

The first European to see Lake Erie, when the Iroquois Indians inhabited the region, was probably the French-Canadian explorer Louis Jolliet, in 1669, although some credit the French man Étienne Brûlé with its exploration as early as 1615. The British, allied with the Iroquois, developed trade along Lake Erie in the late 17th century. British pressure led to the takeover of two strategic French forts, in 1759 (Fort-Conti, thereafter Ft. Niagara) and in 1760 (Fort-Pontchartrain-du-Détroit, thereafter Ft. Detroit). Many British loyalists then moved north of the lake into Ontario, and the American shores were not settled until after 1796. In the Battle of Lake Erie, an important engagement of the War of 1812, U.S. commodore Oliver H. Perry defeated a British squadron at Put-in-Bay, Ohio, and secured the Northwest for the United States. The lake was named after the Erie Indians who once inhabited the shores.

Lake Huron

Lake Huron is the second largest of the Great Lakes of North America, bounded on the west by Michigan (U.S.) and on the north and east by Ontario (Can.). The lake is 331 km (206 miles) long from northwest to southeast, and its maximum width is 294 km (183 miles). The total area of its drainage basin is 133,900 square km (51,700 square miles), exclusive of the lake surface area, which is 59,570 square km (23,000 square miles). Inflow into the lake is received from Lake Superior (via the St. Marys River), from Lake Michigan (via the Straits of Mackinac), and from numerous streams draining the adjacent lands. The lake discharges at its southern end into Lake Erie (via the St. Clair River, Lake St. Clair, and the Detroit River).

With a mean surface height of 176 metres (577 feet) above sea level, the lake reaches a maximum depth of 229 metres (750 feet). Many islands lie in the northeastern part of the lake, notably Manitoulin Island and many others in Georgian Bay and the North Channel. Scenic Mackinac Island and several others are located near the Straits of Mackinac in the northwest part of the lake, and Saginaw Bay indents the Michigan coast.

Lumbering and fishing have been important economic activities in the Lake Huron region, and many resorts line the lake's shores. As part of the St. Lawrence Seaway, the lake supports heavy commercial traffic in iron ore, grain, and limestone. The average navigation season extends from early April to late December. Large tonnages of limestone are loaded at Rockport and Rogers City, Mich. Other harbours important in local trade include Cheboygan, Alpena, Bay City, and Harbor Beach (in Michigan) and Collingwood, Midland, Tiffin, Port McNicoll, and Depot Harbor on Georgian Bay (in Ontario).

Lake Huron was the first of the Great Lakes to be seen by Europeans. The French explorers Samuel de Champlain and Étienne Brûlé travelled up the Ottawa and Mattawa rivers and reached Georgian Bay in 1615. Brûlé traversed the North Channel to the St. Marys River in 1618. A Jesuit mission was established among the Huron Indians at the Wye River (southeastern corner of Georgian Bay) in 1638 and named Sainte-Marie; but it was destroyed by the Iroquois Indians in 1649. After that, the centre of French activities shifted northwestward to the settlement at Sault Ste. Marie on the St. Marys River. Jacques Marquette, the French missionary and explorer, founded a mission at St. Ignace on the Straits of Mackinac in 1671.

Meanwhile, Louis Jolliet, the French-Canadian explorer, canoed down Lake Huron in 1669 before discovering Lake Erie. The French explorer Robert Cavelier, sieur de La Salle, sailing westward from Niagara, traversed Lake Huron in 1679. British penetration of the lower lakes developed strongly in the mid-18th century, leading to the British capture of Fort-Pontchartrain-du-Détroit (Ft. Detroit) in 1760 and Michilimackinac on the Straits of Mackinac (1761). The current boundary between the U.S. and Canada was drawn after the Revolutionary War (1775–83) and was firmly established after the War of 1812. In the latter war, the fort on Mackinac Island (overlooking the

Straits of Mackinac) was taken by the British, but U.S. troops reoccupied it at the close of the war. The lake was named by the French after the Huron Indians.

LAKE MICHIGAN

Lake Michigan is the third largest of the five Great Lakes of North America and the only one lying wholly within the United States. Bordered by the states of Michigan (east and north), Wisconsin (west), Illinois (southwest), and Indiana (southeast), it connects with Lake Huron through the Straits of Mackinac in the north. The lake is 517 km (321 miles) long (north to south); it has a maximum width of 190 km (118 miles) and a drainage basin of about 118,000 square km (45,500 square miles), exclusive of its surface area, which is 57,757 square km (22,300 square miles). With a mean surface elevation of 176 metres (579 feet) above sea level, the lake has a maximum depth of 281 metres (923 feet). Currents are slight, with a generally southward drift along the western side, a northward drift along the eastern side, and at times counterclockwise swirls in the southern basin and around the Beaver Island group in the north.

Approximately 100 streams flow into the lake, only a few of which are of appreciable size. The Manistee, Pere Marquette, White, Muskegon, Grand, Kalamazoo, and St. Joseph rivers enter the lake from the east. The Fox and Menominee rivers flow into Green Bay, a northwestern arm of the lake. The Chicago River flowed into the southwestern end of the lake but was reversed in 1900 so that it now drains through the Chicago Sanitary and Ship Canal into the Des Plaines River at Joliet, Ill. The northern end of the lake contains all of the islands, the largest of which is Beaver Island, Michigan.

The land adjacent to Lake Michigan is low and gently rolling, but wave-cut bluffs of rock occur in many places.

Sand dunes are common along the southeastern shore, notably at the Indiana Dunes National Lakeshore and State Park, where prevailing winds blow sand inland. The moderating influence of the lake accounts for the noted fruit-growing region along its eastern shore.

Lake Michigan is part of the Great Lakes–St. Lawrence Seaway and, thus, handles international commerce. Although ice in the harbours limits navigation from mid-December through mid-April, the open lake rarely freezes over, and railway-car ferry service across the lake is maintained between some ports throughout the year.

The southern end of the lake abuts a great industrial complex centred on Chicago, which consumes large quantities of waterborne raw materials, principally iron ore, coal, and limestone; these are handled at the ports of

Beach along the south shore of Lake Michigan in Indiana Dunes State Park, northern Indiana, with (right) the steel mills of Gary in the background. © Cathy Melloan

Calumet (South Chicago) Harbor in Illinois and at Indiana (East Chicago) Harbor and Gary in Indiana. Some of the iron ore is loaded at Escanaba, Mich., on the lake's northern shore; but most is brought from the Lake Superior region. Milwaukee and Green Bay, Wis., are centres of distribution of coal from Lake Erie ports. Grain is shipped from Milwaukee and Chicago. Other major lake ports include Michigan City (Ind.); Waukegan (Ill.); Kenosha, Racine, and Manitowoc (Wis.); and Manistee, Ludington, Muskegon, Grand Haven, and Benton Harbor (Mich.).

The restocking of lake trout and the introduction of coho salmon have rejuvenated recreational and commercial fishing on the lake while also greatly reducing the population of alewives (small saltwater fish that entered the Great Lakes via the St. Lawrence Seaway and created many problems when large numbers died off in springtime). Although pollution is threatening the ecological balance of the lake, popular summer-resort areas dot its shores.

In 1634 the French explorer Jean Nicolet became the first European to see Lake Michigan. The Jesuit Claude-Jean Allouez began missionary work among the Indians of Green Bay and the Fox River in 1668. The French explorer Louis Jolliet and the French missionary Jacques Marquette mapped the lake's western shore from Green Bay to Chicago in 1673. Robert Cavelier, sieur de La Salle, also of France, brought the first sailing ship to the lake in 1679, but it was lost in a storm on its return eastward with a cargo of furs. La Salle later established a trading post near St. Joseph, Mich. The name of the lake is from the Algonquian Indian term *michigami,* or *misschiganin,* meaning "big lake."

LAKE ONTARIO

The smallest and most easterly of the Great Lakes of North America, Lake Ontario is bounded on the north by

Ontario (Can.) and on the south by New York (U.S.). The lake is roughly elliptical; its major axis, 311 km (193 miles) long, lies nearly east to west, and its greatest width is 85 km (53 miles). The total area of the lake's drainage basin is 64,025 square km (24,720 square miles), exclusive of the lake's surface area, which is 19,011 square km (7,340 square miles). The Niagara River is the main feeder of the lake; others include the Genesee, Oswego, and Black rivers from the south and the Trent River from the north. The 48-km (30-mile)-wide eastern extremity of the lake is crossed by a chain of five islands, where the lake discharges into the St. Lawrence River near Kingston, Ont. With a mean surface elevation of 74 metres (243 feet) above sea level, Lake Ontario has a mean depth of 86 metres (283 feet), and its deepest point is 244 metres (802 feet). A general surface current (13 km [about 8 miles] per day) flows toward the east and is strongest along the south shore. The Welland Canal (navigational) and the Niagara River (natural) serve as connections with Lake Erie to the southwest. Lake Ontario is linked with the New York State Barge Canal at Oswego, N.Y., and with Lake Huron's Georgian Bay via the Trent Canal at Trenton, Ont. The Rideau Canal runs northeastward in Ontario from Kingston to Ottawa.

The land to the north of Lake Ontario spreads out into broad plains, which are intensively farmed. The Niagara Escarpment, or Lake Ridge, extends eastward along the lake's southern shore (3 to 8 miles inland) from the Niagara River to Sodus, N.Y. Industry is concentrated around the port cities of Toronto and Hamilton, Ont., and Rochester, N.Y. Other important ports along the lake include Kingston and Oswego, N.Y. The lake freezes only near the land, and its harbours are icebound from mid-December to mid-April.

Lake Ontario was visited by Étienne Brûlé, a French scout, and by Samuel de Champlain in 1615. The Iroquois

Indians, allies of the British, held the Ontario region; but during the late 17th and early 18th centuries a temporary peace allowed the French to build forts, including Fort-Frontenac (1673), where Kingston now stands. The French and Indian Wars led to British control, and the American Revolution hastened settlement, trade, and shipping in the region.

LAKE SUPERIOR

Lake Superior is the most northwesterly and largest of the five Great Lakes of North America and one of the world's largest bodies of fresh water. Bounded on the east and north by Ontario (Can.), on the west by Minnesota (U.S.), and on the south by Wisconsin and Michigan (U.S.), it discharges into Lake Huron at its eastern end via the St. Marys River. The lake is 563 km (350 miles) long (east to west), and its greatest width is 258 km (160 miles) from north to south. It has a mean surface elevation of 180 metres (600 feet) above sea level and a maximum depth of 406 metres (1,332 feet). The lake's drainage basin is 127,700 square km (49,300 square miles), exclusive of its surface area of 82,100 square km (31,700 square miles).

The lake is so massive and its volume so large that, were it to be emptied at its current rate (with no compensating additions of water), it would take 191 years. Because of its large size (relative to watershed area) and the porous "dam" at its outlet, long-term lake-level fluctuations are much lower than in any of the other Great Lakes—generally less than 1 metre (3 feet). Annual lake-level fluctuations are less than 30 cm (12 inches).

Lake Superior receives water from approximately 200 rivers, of which the largest are the Nipigon (from the north) and the St. Louis (from the west). Other principal

Shore of Lake Superior near the mouth of the Mosquito River in Pictured Rocks National Lakeshore, Upper Peninsula, Michigan, U.S. © Terry Donnelly from TSW—CLICK/Chicago

rivers entering the north shore are the Pigeon, Kaministikwia, Pic, White, and Michipicoten. No large rivers enter the lake from the south; the middle-sized Sturgeon and Tahquamenon rivers are the main south-shore tributaries. Small amounts of water are also diverted into the lake from two places otherwise outside of the watershed—Long Lac and Ogoki—in order to accentuate hydroelectric-power generation at Sault Ste. Marie, Mich., and Niagara Falls. The principal islands in the lake are Isle

Royale, a U.S. national park; the Apostle Islands, near the Wisconsin shore; Michipicoten, on the east side; and St. Ignace, near the mouth of the Nipigon River (Can.).

The coastline of Lake Superior is picturesque, particularly the north shore, which is indented by deep bays backed by high cliffs. Much of the coastal area is sparsely settled. Extensive forests, which dominate the watershed, are held in federal, state, provincial, and private timberlands. Seasonal hunting, sportfishing, and tourism form the basis for an important regional recreation industry. Valuable mineral deposits surround the lake. Iron ore was mined and smelted locally from 1848, and the opening (1855) of the Soo Locks ship canal on the St. Marys River facilitated iron mining in the region by allowing regular shipment to the lower lakes. Subsequently, iron was extracted from many parts of the Lake Superior district, including the Marquette Range in Michigan and the Mesabi Range in Minnesota. Only taconite and other low-grade ores are now mined and enriched on site. Other minerals extracted include silver (near Thunder Bay, Ont.), nickel (north of the lake), and copper (south of the lake). In the late 1800s a small "gold rush" took place on its southern shore in Michigan.

Lake Superior has many natural harbours, and improvements have created additional ports. The navigation season is generally about eight months long. At Thunder Bay, grain from the Canadian prairies is transferred from rail to ship. Iron ore is exported from Taconite Harbor and Two Harbors (Minn.) and from Marquette (Mich.). The harbour shared by Duluth (Minn.) and Superior (Wis.) is a shipping point for iron ore, grain, and flour. The principal ports along the lake's south shore are Ashland (Wis.), Hancock and Houghton (both on a 25-mi-long canal across the Keweenaw Peninsula, Mich.), and Marquette (Mich.).

Marquette Harbor Lighthouse on Lake Superior, Marquette, Mich. Dale Fisher, U.S. Army Corps of Engineers

All boat traffic that leaves the lake for southern ports must pass through the Soo Locks at Sault Ste. Marie.

The first European to see Lake Superior was probably the French explorer Étienne Brûlé in 1622. Pierre Espirit Radisson and Médard Chouart des Groseilliers gathered a valuable cargo of furs during their extensive travels on the lake (1659–60). The French Jesuit missionary Claude-Jean Allouez circumnavigated and charted the lake in 1667. Daniel Greysolon, sieur (lord) DuLhut (or Du Luth), opened the lake to active trading in 1679. French fur trading then flourished at intervals, but the entire region came under British control between 1763 and 1783. Trade remained in the hands of the British until 1817, when John Jacob Astor's American Fur Company took over south of the Canadian border. The lake's name is from the French Lac Supérieur ("Upper Lake").

LAKE AGASSIZ

Lake Agassiz was the largest of the ice-margin lakes that once covered what are now parts of Manitoba, Ontario, and Saskatchewan in Canada and North Dakota and Minnesota in the United States. It was present in the Pleistocene Epoch (approximately 2.6 million to 11,700 years ago) during the last two phases of the Wisconsin glacial age, when the Laurentide Ice Sheet blocked the drainage of the northern Great Plains into what is today Hudson Bay. As a result, the waters of the Saskatchewan and other rivers backed up, forming the 1,100-km (700-mile)-long by 300-km (200-mile)-wide Lake Agassiz and the smaller lakes of Souris and Saskatchewan, which drained through various outlets (depending upon their water level) either into the Mississippi River (via the Minnesota River) or Lake Superior. With the retreat of the ice sheet after nearly 1,000 years, a channel to the north (now the Nelson River) drained the 285,000-square-km (110,000-square-mile) Lake Agassiz into Hudson Bay, leaving Lakes Winnipeg, Winnipegosis, and Manitoba and Lake of the Woods as remnants. The fine claylike silt that accumulated on the bottom of Agassiz is responsible for the fertility of the valleys of the Red and Souris rivers. The lake was named in 1879 after the Swiss-born naturalist and geologist Louis Agassiz, who conducted extensive studies on the movement of glaciers.

GREAT SALT LAKE

The Great Salt Lake is located in northern Utah, U.S. It is the largest inland body of salt water in the Western Hemisphere and one of the most saline inland bodies of water in the world. The lake is fed by the Bear, Weber, and Jordan rivers and has no outlet. The lake has fluctuated greatly in size, depending on the rates of evaporation and the flow of the rivers that feed it. Its surface area has varied from about 6,200 square km (2,400 square miles) at its highest levels in 1873 and the mid-1980s to about 2,460 square km (950 square miles) at its lowest level in 1963. At high level the lake's surface is 1,284 metres (4,212 feet) above sea level, and at low level it is 1,277 metres (4,191 feet). At times of median water level, the lake is generally less than 4.5 metres (15 feet) deep, with a maximum depth of 11 metres (35 feet).

Like the Dead Sea, the Great Salt Lake exists within an arid environment and has chemical characteristics similar to that of the oceans. It has a much greater salinity than the oceans, however, since natural evaporation exceeds the supply of water from the rivers feeding the lake.

Surrounded by great stretches of sand, salt land, and marsh, the Great Salt Lake remains eerily isolated from the nearby cities, towns, and other human habitations, though in recent years means have been found to turn its apparent sterility to a profit in both economic and recreational terms. It has become important not only as a source of minerals but also as a beach and water-sports attraction and a wildlife preserve.

The Great Salt Lake is the largest of the lake remnants of prehistoric freshwater Lake Bonneville, the others being Bear Lake, on the Utah-Idaho border, and Utah Lake, west of Provo, Utah. Formed late in the Pleistocene Epoch about 30,000 years ago, Lake Bonneville at high water covered almost 52,000 square km (20,000 square miles) of present-day western Utah and also extended into modern Nevada and Idaho. During succeeding glacial periods, large quantities of fresh water entered this intermontane basin and drained out through the Snake River—ultimately into the Columbia River and the Pacific Ocean. During the interglacial and postglacial periods, however, water levels decreased and the outflows were cut off. Water, therefore, could escape only through evaporation, and the mineral salts from the inflowing rivers remained trapped in the lake.

The lake appeared on 18th-century maps of the continent through reports of explorer-trappers and Indian tales as a semilegendary body alternately named Timpanogos or Buenaventura, depending on the source. The first white explorers whose accounts are fully credited were the trappers Étienne Provost and Jim Bridger, who came upon the lake independently in 1824–25. More detailed investigations were made by Captain John C. Frémont in 1843 and 1845. The Mormons' settlement in 1847 of their "promised land," on the nearby site of Salt Lake City, brought the region more fully into national awareness. The lake was surveyed in 1850, and in 1869 the last spike of America's first transcontinental railroad was driven near the lake's northeastern shore. The study of the Great Basin region by the U.S. Geological Survey in 1890 was an important source of information about the lake, and later studies have been led by that agency.

The lake's basin is defined by the foothills of the Wasatch Range to the north, east, and south and by the Great Salt Lake Desert, a remnant of the bed of Lake Bonneville, to the west. The part of this desert known as the Bonneville Salt Flats has become an automobile raceway, the site of many trials for world land-speed records. The lake's varying shoreline consists of beaches, marshes, and mudflats. The 48-km (30-mile)-long Lucin Cutoff, an east-west causeway laid down for a rail line in 1959, connects the cities of Ogden and Lucin, splits the lake, and affects the water level. Because the lake's main tributaries enter from the south, the water level of the southern section is several inches higher than that of the northern part. Eleven small islands, the largest of which are Antelope and Fremont, lie south of the cutoff. The Great Salt Lake's record high levels in the mid-1980s threatened the Lucin Cutoff, highways, and sewage-treatment plants along the shore, and in 1987 pumps were installed that began draining some of the lake's excess waters into the Great Salt Lake Desert to the west. The resulting new body of water was called the Newfoundland Evaporation Basin.

The Bear, Weber, and Jordan rivers carry more than 1.1 million tons of salts annually into the lake. The total dissolved mineral accumulation in the lake basin is some 5 billion tons, mainly sodium and chloride, though sulfate, magnesium, and potassium also are abundant. Table salt and potash production from brines dates from the 19th century, while magnesium production on a large scale began only in 1971.

The high salt content makes the lake itself uninhabitable for all but a few minor forms of life, such as brine shrimp. The marshes, mudflats, and islands, however, attract much waterfowl, including pelicans, herons, cormorants, terns, and gulls, while Antelope Island has been made a refuge for bison.

GREAT SLAVE LAKE

Great Slave Lake is located in the east-central Fort Smith region, Northwest Territories, Canada, near the Alberta border. It was named for the Slave Indians. The lake was visited in 1771 by the English explorer Samuel Hearne; it was not completely surveyed, however, until the early 1920s. Fed by several rivers, of which the Slave is most important, and drained by the Mackenzie into the Arctic Ocean, the lake, with an area of 28,568 square km (11,030 square miles), is the fifth largest in North America. It is 500 km (300 miles) long and 50–225 km (30–140 miles) wide and has a shoreline indented by large bays, often with rocky slopes. Its waters are extremely clear and deep (maximum depth more than 600 metres [2,000 feet]).

The lake contains many islands and supports a fishing industry (trout and whitefish) based at the villages of Hay River and Gros Cap. The lake, linking the Mackenzie and Slave rivers, is an integral part of the Mackenzie River waterway, though ice-free for only four months.

LAKE BAIKAL

Lake Baikal (Russian: Ozero Baykal, also spelled Ozero Bajkal) is a body of water located in the southern part of eastern Siberia within the republic of Buryatia and Irkutsk *oblast* (province) of Russia. It is the oldest existing freshwater lake on Earth (20–25 million years old), as well as the deepest continental body of water, having a maximum depth of 1,620 metres (5,315 feet). Its area is some 31,500 square km (12,200 square miles), with a length of 636 km (395 miles) and an average width of 48 km (30 miles). It is also the world's largest freshwater lake by volume, containing about one-fifth of the fresh water on the Earth's surface, some 23,000 cubic km (5,500 cubic miles). Into Lake Baikal flow more than 330 rivers and streams, the largest of which include the Selenga, Barguzin, Upper (Verkhnyaya) Angara, Chikoy, and Uda.

Ice-clad Lake Baikal and its only outlet, the Angara River, at Irkutsk, Russia. Hulton Archive/Getty Images

Baikal lies in a deep structural hollow surrounded by mountains, some of which rise more than 2,000 metres (6,600 feet) above the lake's surface. The sedimentary strata on the floor of the lake may be as much as 6,100 metres (20,000 feet) thick. Breaks in the Earth's crust produce hot mineral springs in the area. There are occasional severe earthquakes; in 1862 a quake inundated about 200 square km (77 square miles) in the northern Selenga delta, creating a new bay in Baikal known as Proval Bay.

The lake hollow is not symmetrical, having steep slopes on the western shores and gentler slopes on the eastern. The meandering shoreline runs for some 2,100 km (1,300 miles), with large indentations at the bays of Barguzin, Chivyrkuysky, and Proval and at Ayaya and Frolikha inlets; the Svyatoy Nos Peninsula juts out into the lake from the eastern shore. Baikal contains some 45 islets and islands, the largest of which are Olkhon (about 700 square km [270 square miles]) and Bolshoy (Great) Ushkany (9.4 square km [3.6 square miles]). The influx of water into the lake is primarily from rivers, chiefly the Selenga. The only outflow is through the Angara River, a tributary of the Yenisey.

Baikal's climate is much milder than that of the surrounding territory. Winter air temperatures average -21 °C (-6 °F), and August temperatures average 11 °C (52 °F). The lake surface freezes in January and thaws in May or June. The water temperature at the surface in August is between 10 and 12 °C (50 and 54 °F) and reaches 20 °C (68 °F) in the offshore shallows. Waves can be as high as 4.6 metres (15 feet). The water is very clear; from the surface one can see to 40 metres (130 feet). Its salinity is low, and it contains few minerals.

Plant and animal life in the lake is rich and various. There are between 1,500 and 1,800 animal species at different depths, and hundreds of plant species live on or

Baikal seals (Phoca sibirica), endemic to Lake Baikal, southeastern Siberia, Russia. © Doug Allan/Oxford Scientific Films Ltd.

near the surface. The majority of the species are endemic to Baikal. There are some 50 species of fish, belonging to seven families; the most numerous of these are the 25 species of gobies. The omul salmon is heavily fished; also important are the grayling, lake whitefish, and sturgeon. Unique to the lake is a fish called the golomyanka, of the family Comephoridae, which gives birth to live young. The one mammal species is the Baikal seal, or nerpa (*Phoca sibirica*). There are more than 320 bird species in the Baikal area.

Industries along the shores of Baikal include mining (mica and marble), the manufacture of cellulose and paper, shipbuilding, fisheries, and timber. There are many mineral springs, and visitors come to Goryachinsk for the curative properties of the waters. A pulp and paper mill built on Lake Baikal's southern shore in 1966 drew strong environmental protests from Soviet scientists and writers because its wastes were polluting the water, and in 1971 the Soviet government adopted a decree to protect the lake from polluting emissions. Further pollution controls were resisted, however, and industrial waste at the site remained a concern in the late 1990s.

The Limnological Institute of the Siberian Division of the Russian Academy of Sciences is located in the town of Listvyanka, as is the Baikal Sanatorium, and the hydrobiological station of Irkutsk State University is in Bolshiye Koty (Bolshoy Koti). The protection of natural resources in the area began with the establishment of the Barguzinsky Nature Reserve in 1916; subsequently there were added the Baikalsky (1969) and Baikalo-Lenskiy (1986) nature reserves, the Frolikhinskiy (1976) and Kabansky (1974) wildlife reserves, and the Zabaikalsky and Pribaikalsky national parks (both 1986). The Lake Baikal Coastal Protection Zone, covering the lake and its environs (a total of 88,000 square km [34,000 square miles]), was created in 1987, and the same area was designated a UNESCO World Heritage site in 1996.

LAKE BALKHASH

Lake Balkhash (Kazak: Balqash) is a lake situated in east-central Kazakhstan. It lies in the vast Balqash-Alaköl basin at 342 metres (1,122 feet) above sea level and is situated 966 km (600 miles) east of the Aral Sea. It is 605 km (376 miles) long from west to east. Its area varies within significant limits, depending on the water balance. In years in which there is an abundance of water (as at the beginning of the 20th century and in the decade 1958–69), the lake's area reaches 18,000–19,000 square km (6,900–7,300 square miles). In drought-afflicted periods, however (as at the end of the 19th century and in the 1930s and '40s), the area of the lake decreases to 15,500–16,300 square km (6,000–6,300 square miles). Such changes in area are accompanied by changes in the water level of about 3 metres (10 feet). Jutting far out into the lake is the Sarymsek Peninsula, which divides Balkhash into two separate hydrologic parts: a western part, wide and shallow, and an eastern part, narrow and relatively deep. Accordingly, the width of the lake changes from 74 to 27 km (46 to 17 miles) in the western part and 10 to 19 km (6 to 12 miles) in the eastern part. The depth of the western part does not exceed 11 metres (36 feet), whereas the eastern part reaches 26 metres (85 feet). The two parts of the lake are united by a narrow strait, the Uzynaral, with a depth of about 6 metres (21 feet).

The large Ile River, flowing in from the south, spills into the western part of the lake, and it contributed 80–90 percent of the total influx into the lake until a hydroelectric project reduced the volume of the river's inflow late in the 20th century. Only such small rivers as the Qaratal, Aqsū, Ayaguz, and Lepsi feed the eastern part of the lake. With almost equal areas in both parts of the lake, this situation creates a continuous flow of water from the western to the eastern section. The water of the western part was almost fresh and suitable for industrial use and consumption, but that of the eastern part has long been salty.

The north banks of the lake are high and rocky, with clear-cut traces of ancient terraces. The south banks are low and sandy, and wide belts of them are covered with thickets of reeds and numerous small lakes. These low-lying banks are periodically flooded by the waters of the lake.

Harsh climatic conditions prevail, and the warm summers and cold winters significantly affect the whole regime of the lake. The average annual water temperature in the western part of the lake is 10 °C (50 °F); in the eastern part it is 9 °C (48 °F). Average precipitation is approximately 430 mm (17 inches). The lake remains frozen from the end of November to the beginning of April.

Carbonates predominate in the ground deposits of the lake. The fauna of the lake was formerly rich but declined from the 1970s owing to the lake's deteriorating water quality. Before these declines began, 20 species of fish inhabited the lake, of which six were peculiar to the lake itself. The remainder had been introduced to the lake and include the sazan, sturgeon, eastern bream, pike, and Aral barbel. The main food fish were the sazan, pike, and Balqash perch.

The economic importance of Lake Balkhash had greatly increased during the first part of the 20th century. Most significant was the fishing and fish breeding begun in the 1930s. A regular shipping service with a large freight turnover also developed. Also of great economic significance to the region was the construction of the Balqash copper-refining plant, around which the large city of Balqash grew on the north shore of the lake. However, in 1970 the Qapshaghay hydroelectric-power station began operations on the Ile River. The diversion of water to fill the Qapshaghay reservoir and to provide for irrigation reduced the flow of the Ile River by two-thirds and caused a decline in the lake's water level. The surface of Lake Balkhash dropped 2.2 metres (7 feet) between 1970 and 1987. The lake has become increasingly saline and has also suffered pollution from the leakage of fuel-storage depots and from copper mining and processing along its shores. Much of the catch from the fishing industry is now quarantined, and the forest and wetland habitats around the lake have shrunk. As of the early 1990s, no action had been taken to reverse the ecological damage done to the lake and its surroundings.

LAKE CHAD

Lake Chad (French: Lac Tchad) is a freshwater lake located in the Sahelian zone of west-central Africa at the conjunction of Chad, Cameroon, Nigeria, and Niger. It is situated in an interior basin formerly occupied by a much larger ancient sea that is sometimes called Mega-Chad. Historically, Lake Chad has ranked among the largest lakes in Africa, though its surface area varies greatly by season, as well as from year to year. When the surface of the lake is approximately 280 metres (920 feet) above sea level, the area is about 17,800 square km (6,875 square miles); in the early 21st century, however, the area was typically about 1,500 square km (580 square miles). The hydrologic contributions and biological diversity of Lake Chad are important regional assets. The region is noteworthy for important archaeological discoveries, its role in trans-Saharan trade, and its association with historic African kingdoms.

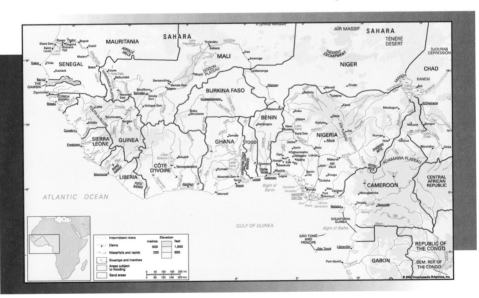

The Niger and Sénégal river basins, the Lake Chad basin, and their drainage networks. Encyclopaedia Britannica, Inc.

GEOLOGY AND PHYSIOGRAPHY

The Chad basin is a downwarped section of the Precambrian African Shield. Most of the older crystalline rocks are covered by more recent deposits. The most significant physiographic influence on the basin was the ancient sea. At its maximum extent the sea was more than 180 metres (600 feet) deep, occupied an area of approximately 400,000 square km (154,400 square miles), and drained into the Atlantic Ocean through the Benue River system. It experienced four high stages between 41,000 and 2,300 years ago. The history of the sea is documented in the stratigraphic record, which includes thick layers of diatomaceous earth, lacustrine sands, terraced shorelines, and the remains of modern fish and mollusks in now-arid tracts of the basin. The floor of the basin dips to the northeast of the modern lake, reaching its lowest point in the Djourab Depression, some 480 km (300 miles) away. Lake Chad occasionally overflows into the generally intermittent El-Ghazal River leading into the depression, but it is usually confined by the dune fields of Kanem.

CLIMATE

The climate of the Lake Chad region is strongly influenced by the seasonal migration and interaction of the dominant air masses of the region: a dry, subsiding continental air mass and a humid, unstable maritime air mass. The humid air mass moves northward during the summer, wedging beneath the drier air mass. Precipitation occurs when the depth of humid air is sufficiently great. The depth of the air mass varies daily as well as seasonally, accounting for variation in precipitation levels. At the end of the summer the dominance of the dry continental air mass is reasserted. Evaporation and transpirational losses from soil and plants increase, and then they decrease as the surface layers of the soil dry and plants lose their leaves. The dry season is also the period of the harmattan, a dust-laden wind that reduces visibility for days at a time. The increased insolation, reduced humidity, and desiccating winds contribute greatly to water loss in the lake.

Precipitation levels are greatest from July to September. Annual precipitation averages 560 mm (22 inches) at the southern margin of Lake Chad and about 250 mm (10 inches) at the northern margin. Variability during the year is high and increases from south to north; variability from year to year is also high, and droughts are frequent. Temperatures during the wet season are moderate, with highs above 32 °C (90 °F). In October and November, during the transition to the dry season, daily highs again rise above 32 °C (90 °F), and diurnal ranges are almost double those of the wet season. During December and January daytime highs are lower, with nighttime lows sometimes falling to about 8 °C (46 °F). April is usually the hottest month of the year, with temperatures occasionally reaching above 43 °C (110 °F).

HYDROLOGY

Lake Chad is a variable body of water. Its measured surface area typically fluctuates seasonally, peaking in late October or early November, then shrinking by more than half by late April or early May. The lake is dotted with numerous islands, which can coalesce into larger land areas during periods of extremely low surface levels. The volume of the lake reflects local precipitation and the discharge of its catchment area, balanced against losses through evaporation, transpiration, and seepage. The lake is fed chiefly by the Chari (Shari)-Logone river system, which accounts for about four-fifths of the inflow. Of the remaining inflow, most is contributed by the Ebeji (El-Béid) and Yedseram rivers. Losses to evaporation and the transpiration of aquatic plants amount to approximately 100 inches (2,500 mm) each year. It is probable that up to another 10 inches (250 mm) replenish groundwater supplies in the adjacent Manga and Kanem lowlands and pass as underflow through the El-Ghazal.

At times when the lake has a greater surface area, it can be divided into two pools partially separated by a low ridge extending roughly northeast-southwest across the centre of the lake; the ridge was formed during a drought at the beginning of the 20th century, and at times it has completely divided the basins. Typically, depths of 4 to 7 metres (13 to 23 feet) are common in the northwestern pool, and 10-metre (33-foot) depths can occur among the islands along the eastern margin of the pool. Because of sediment deposition by the Chari River, the southeastern pool is generally shallower—3 to 4 metres (10 to 13 feet) deep—but sometimes reaches depths of 11 metres (36 feet) along the archipelago. The gentle slope of the lakeshore allows persistent dry-season winds to locally affect water levels for short periods of time. The salt content of Lake Chad is unusually low for a tropical dryland lake with no outlet. As the waters of the lake evaporate during the dry season, the salt content increases, with the highest values recorded along the northeastern shoreline.

Travelers reported high water levels and overflow into the El-Ghazal during the 13th and 19th centuries. In 1870, for example, Lake Chad covered some 28,000 square km (10,800 square miles). At the turn of the 20th century the lake began to diminish in size, but by the 1920s it had recovered, and in 1956 it again overflowed into the El-Ghazal. During the 1970s and '80s the amplitude of the lake's annual variability was the highest recorded in the 20th century, with average levels falling below long-term norms; the surface area was reduced to less than 3,900 square km (1,500 square miles) for a time in the mid-1980s and again in the early 21st century. The corresponding variability in rainfall appears to have been related to the effects of environmental degradation.

PLANT LIFE

The well-drained soils around Lake Chad once supported a relatively dense woodland, including species such as kapok and ebony. Changing patterns of land use and progressive degradation have reduced diversity and resulted in a more open woodland increasingly composed of species adapted to reduced moisture. They include several acacias, baobab, desert date, palms, African myrrh, and Indian jujube. The periodically inundated lands near the lake are more heavily vegetated. Annual grasses are increasing at the expense of the more economically valuable perennial species. Papyrus, ambatch, water lilies, and reeds dominate aquatic vegetation.

ANIMAL LIFE

Visitors to the medieval kingdom of Kanem in the Lake Chad region described an abundance of wildlife; until the early 20th century essentially the same faunal assemblages were reported. Since then, however, habitat loss, hunting, and direct competition from livestock have depleted wildlife populations. As with vegetation, the trend is toward decreased diversity and lower levels of biological productivity. Large carnivores, including lions and leopards, have been eliminated in livestock areas; and other large animals such as rhinoceroses and hippopotamuses have been reduced or eliminated. Nocturnal species have been less affected by these changes; and some, particularly rodents, have benefited from them.

Hundreds of species of birds reside permanently or seasonally in the Lake Chad region. Included are prominent terrestrial birds—such as ostriches, secretary birds, Nubian bustards, and ground hornbills—and the water and shore birds for which the region is famous—such as the garganeys, shovelers, fulvous tree ducks, Egyptian geese, pink-backed pelicans, marabou storks, glossy ibises, and African spoonbills. Included among the amphibians and reptiles are Nile crocodiles, rock pythons, and spitting cobras. The Chad basin remains an important fishery, with more than 40 species of commercial importance. Also noteworthy are such ancient species as the lungfish and sailfin.

Secretary bird (Sagittarius serpentarius). © Stephen J. Krasemann/Peter Arnold, Inc.

Study and Exploration

For millennia, settlement patterns of peoples of Mediterranean and sub-Saharan origin have overlapped in the Sahara, and there is emerging evidence of a long history of interaction between the Lake Chad region and other regions of northern Africa. There are essentially four periods during which the region was strongly affected by external influences. The first is expressed in hints of Egyptian contact with the region, in the sub-Saharan commerce of Carthage and the Garamantes, and in references in Greek, Roman, and Arabic literature. The second period was precipitated largely by the expansion of Islam in North Africa during the 7th century CE, when groups of Arabs and Imazighen (Berbers) who resisted conversion sought refuge in the dry lands of the south. The third period emerged from trade between Kanem or Bornu and Mediterranean Africa, the penetration of Islam into sub-Saharan Africa, and increased Arab interest in geographic exploration. It is documented in the many Arabic works written in the 9th to 14th centuries and is also reflected in Abraham Cresque's *Catalan Atlas* (c. 1375). The fourth period emerged from growing interest in Africa within European academic and commercial circles and was a prelude to European colonization. Numerous descriptions of the Lake Chad region were written by 19th-century Europeans, and three scientific missions were mounted between 1898 and 1909.

Since the 1960s the region has been the subject of long-term climatological studies. In 1964 the Lake Chad Basin Commission (LCBC) was formed by Cameroon, Chad, Niger, and Nigeria; the Central African Republic joined in 1994. The LCBC is charged with regulating the use of the waters of the lake and the basin for the development of livestock, crop, fishery, and water resources. It has also attempted to find ways to reverse the drastic decline in the size of the lake.

LAKE NYASA

Lake Nyasa, which is also called Lake Malawi, is the southernmost and third largest of the East African Rift Valley lakes of East Africa, lying in a deep trough mainly within Malawi. The existence of the lake was reported by a Portuguese explorer, Caspar Boccaro, in 1616. David Livingstone, the British explorer-missionary, reached it from the south in 1859.

The lake's middle line and its northern and eastern shores form much of Malawi's boundary with Tanzania and Mozambique. Its north-south length is 584 km (363 miles); its width varies from 16 to 80 km (10 to 50 miles); and its area is 29,604 square km (11,430 square miles). The surface of the lake is 472 metres (1,550 feet) above sea level, and the depth increases to 704 metres (2,310 feet) toward the northern end, where the forested Livingstone Mountains to the east and the Nyika Plateau and Viphya Mountains to the west fall precipitously down to the lakeshore.

A fresh southeasterly wind (the *mwera*) prevails from May to August, causing short gales and restless waters; the coastline offers little shelter. Halfway up the lake is Likoma Island, a mission headquarters and site of an imposing Anglican cathedral (completed 1911). On the heavily populated Malawi shore there are government stations at Mangochi, Nkhotakota, Nkhata Bay, and Karonga.

Nyasa (meaning "lake") is fed by 14 perennial rivers, the largest being the Ruhuhu; the sole outlet is the Shire River, a tributary of the Zambezi. Hundreds of species of fish have been recorded in the lake, many of which are endemic, being isolated from the Zambezi fauna by the

Murchison Falls. Commercial fisheries exist at the southern end of the lake, based chiefly on the freshwater fish *Tilapia*; fly hatches on the lake occur in clouds large enough to obscure the horizon. Increased environmental degradation has had adverse effects on wildlife in the lake, however; excessive silting disrupts fish feeding and breeding grounds, reducing their numbers. In addition, overfishing, the use of nets with a mesh size smaller than those recommended by fisheries experts, and the disregard of the ban on fishing in the breeding season has also had a detrimental effect on fish populations there.

Passenger and cargo vessels are operated by the Malawi Railways company; Monkey Bay, Nkhotakota, Nkhata Bay, Likoma Island, Chilumba, and Karonga are the main ports. Cotton, rubber, rice, tung oil, and peanuts (groundnuts) are shipped to the railhead at Chipoka in the south, from which point the railway connects through the city of Limbe with Beira, Mozam.

LAKE TANGANYIKA

Lake Tanganyika is the second largest of the lakes of eastern Africa. It is the longest freshwater lake in the world (660 km [410 miles]) and the second deepest (1,436 metres [4,710 feet]) after Lake Baikal in Russia. Comparatively narrow, varying in width from 16 to 72 km (10 to 45 miles), it covers about 32,900 square km (12,700 square miles) and forms the boundary between Tanzania and Congo (Kinshasa). It occupies the southern end of the Western Rift Valley, and for most of its length the land rises steeply from its shores. Its waters tend to be brackish. Though fed by a number of rivers, the lake is not the centre of an extensive drainage area. The largest rivers discharging into the lake are the Malagarasi, the Ruzizi, and the Kalambo, which has one of the highest waterfalls in the world (215 metres [704 feet]). Its outlet is the Lukuga River, which flows into the Lualaba River.

Lake Tanganyika is situated on the line dividing the floral regions of eastern and western Africa, and oil palms, which are characteristic of the flora of western Africa, grow along the lake's shores. Rice and subsistence crops are grown along the shores, and fishing is of some significance. Hippopotamuses and crocodiles abound, and the bird life is varied.

Many of the numerous peoples (predominantly Bantu-speaking) living on the lake's eastern borders trace their origins to areas in the Congo River basin. The lake was first visited by Europeans in 1858, when the British explorers Sir Richard Burton and John Hanning Speke reached Ujiji, on the lake's eastern shore, in their quest for the source of the Nile River. In 1871 Henry (later Sir Henry)

Lake Tanganyika near Bujumbura, Burundi Kay Honkanen/Ostman Agency

Morton Stanley "found" David Livingstone at Ujiji. Important ports situated along Lake Tanganyika are Bujumbura (Burundi), Kalemi (Congo), and Ujiji and Kigoma (Tanzania).

LAKE VICTORIA

Lake Victoria, which is also called Victoria Nyanza, is the largest lake in Africa and chief reservoir of the Nile, lying mainly in Tanzania and Uganda but bordering on Kenya. Among the freshwater lakes of the world it is exceeded in size only by Lake Superior in North America, its area being 69,484 square km (26,828 square miles). An irregular quadrilateral in shape, its shores, save on the west, are deeply indented. Its greatest length from north to south is 337 km (210 miles), its greatest breadth 240 km (150 miles). Its coastline exceeds 3,220 km (2,000 miles). Its waters fill a shallow depression in the centre of the great plateau that stretches between the Western and Eastern Rift Valleys. The lake's surface is 1,134 metres (3,720 feet) above sea level, and its greatest ascertained depth is 82 metres (270 feet). Many archipelagos are contained within the lake, as are numerous reefs, often just below the surface of the clear waters. Lake Victoria has more than 200 species of fish, of which the *Tilapia* is the most economically important. The lake's basin area covers 238,900 square km (92,240 square miles).

The lake's shores vary in aspect. The lake's southwestern coast is backed by precipices 90 metres (300 feet) high, which give way on the western coast to papyrus and ambatch swamps marking the delta of the Kagera River. The lake's deeply indented northern coast is flat and bare. A narrow channel leads into the Kavirondo Gulf, which has an average width of 25 km

(16 miles) and extends for 64 km (40 miles) eastward to Kisumu, Kenya. The Ugandan cities of Kampala and Entebbe lie along or near the northern coast. At the lake's southeastern corner is Speke Gulf, and at the southwestern corner Emin Pasha Gulf. Of the numerous islands in the lake, Ukerewe, north of Speke Gulf, is the largest, with wooded hills rising 200 metres (650 feet) above the lake. It is densely populated. At the lake's northwestern corner are the 62 islands of the Sese archipelago, some of them of striking beauty.

The Kagera River, the largest and most important of the lake affluents, enters the western side of Lake Victoria just north of latitude 1° S. The only other river of note entering from the west is the Katonga, north of Kagera. The lake's only outlet is the Victoria Nile, which exits from the northern coast.

The search by Europeans for the source of the Nile led to the sighting of the lake by the British explorer John Hanning Speke in 1858. Formerly known to the Arabs as Ukerewe, the lake was named by Speke in honour of Queen Victoria of England. A detailed survey of the lake was made by Sir William Garstin in 1901. Plans for gradually raising the level of the lake's waters were completed in 1954 with the construction of the Owen Falls Dam (now the Nalubaale Dam) on the Victoria Nile at Jinja, Ugan.; the dam, which provides hydroelectric power on a large scale, made the lake a vast reservoir. A second dam, Kiira, was later constructed 1 km (0.6 mile) from Nalubaale. It was completed in 1999 and began producing hydroelectric power the next year.

The Lake Victoria region is one of the most densely populated in Africa; within 80 km (50 miles) of its shores live several million people, nearly all Bantu-speaking. There are local steamer services around the lake.

LAKE WINNIPEG

Lake Winnipeg is a large water body located in south-central Manitoba, Canada, at the southwestern edge of the Canadian Shield, the rocky, glaciated region of eastern Canada. Fed by many rivers, including the Saskatchewan, Red, and Winnipeg, which drain a large part of the Great Plains, the lake is drained to the northeast by the Nelson River into Hudson Bay. Lake Winnipeg, at an altitude of 217 metres (713 feet), is 425 km (264 miles) long and up to 109 km (68 miles) wide. It has an area of 24,387 square km (9,416 square miles) and is one of Canada's largest freshwater lakes.

Visited in the 1730s by the son of La Vérendrye (the French voyageur) and named from the Cree Indian words for "muddy water," the lake is a remnant of glacial Lake Agassiz. With an average depth of about 15 metres (50 feet) — 217 metres (713 feet) at its deepest point — it is important for shipping and commercial fishing (based at Gimli), while its southern shore is a major resort area serving Winnipeg, 64 km (40 miles) south. Major islands include Hecla, Deer, and Black, which form part of Hecla Provincial Park (862 square km [333 square miles]).

CHAPTER 5
WETLANDS

Wetlands are terrestrial ecosystems characterized by poor drainage and the consequent presence most or all of the time of sluggishly moving or standing water saturating the soil. They are usually classified, according to soil and plant life, as bog, marsh, or swamp. Wetlands occur along marine coasts and in areas far removed from the oceans and their influence. Because wetlands occur at the interface of a body of water and the land, they are examples of boundary ecosystems.

COASTAL SYSTEMS

Wetlands in coastal areas can be classified into three basic types: mangroves, salt marshes, and freshwater tidal marshes. Other important coastal systems not formally considered wetlands but found at the boundary between land and water are seaweed-based systems, sea-grass beds, and coastal mudflats.

The fundamental characteristics of shoreline ecosystems are determined by the amount of energy in the water available to move sediments. This energy is supplied by wind-driven currents, tidal currents, and wave action. In high-energy areas the fine sediment is carried away, leaving bedrock, boulders, or cobbles. This creates a prime habitat for seaweeds. As the energy level of water movement progressively lessens, sediments ranging from pebbles to sand, silt, and mud can settle and remain in place. Soft sediments provide a suitable habitat for salt marshes or mangrove forests between tide marks and for sea grasses below the low-tide mark. On a coastline consisting of alternating headlands and embayments, the headlands are most likely to be exposed to strong wave action and to be inhabited by seaweed communities, while the sheltered embayments are more likely to have soft sediments with rooted plant communities. The characteristics of shoreline communities are discussed according to the type of plant production on which they are based.

MANGROVE SWAMPS

Mangrove swamps are found along tropical and subtropical coastlines throughout the world, usually between 25° N and 25° S latitude. The mangrove swamp is an association of halophytic trees, shrubs, and other plants growing in brackish to saline tidal waters of tropical and subtropical coastlines. This coastal forested wetland (called a "mangal" by some researchers) is infamous for its impenetrable maze of woody vegetation, unconsolidated peat, and many adaptations to the double stresses of flooding

Black mangroves (Avicennia germinans), a species native to Florida.
Thomas Eisner

and salinity. Approximately 68 species of mangrove trees exist in the world. Their uneven distribution is thought to be related to continental drift and possibly to transport by primitive humans. Mangrove swamps are dominant particularly in the Indo-West Pacific region, where they have the greatest diversity of species—30 to 40 species of mangroves, compared with about 10 species in the Americas.

In the tropics and subtropics the intertidal areas of soft sediment are usually colonized by mangrove trees. Beneath them lies a waterlogged mixture of mud and decaying mangrove leaves that has very little oxygen; an aboveground root system allows the trees to take in air. This network of aerial roots forms a tangled mass that traps sediment but makes a mangrove forest very difficult for large animals (or humans) to penetrate. Small seaweeds and microscopic algae grow on the trunks and roots of the mangroves, and microscopic algae grow on the surface of the mud. This substrate, along with the decaying mangrove leaves, supports a rich and diverse animal community. Crabs and shrimps are often abundant, and clams and snails of many kinds abound. Mudskippers (family Periophthalmidae), which are fish that have developed the capability of leaving the water and moving over the mud surface in pursuit of prey, are found in mangrove systems, as is the mud lobster (*Thalassina anomala*), which lives in burrows. Because the plankton of adjacent coastal waters is often relatively unproductive, the productivity of the mangrove forests is an important element of the productivity of the whole coastal zone.

SALT MARSHES

Along intertidal shores in middle and high latitudes throughout the world, salt marshes replace the mangrove swamps of tropical and subtropical coastlines. These marshes flourish wherever the accumulation of sediments is equal to or greater than the rate of land subsidence and where there is adequate protection from destructive waves and storms. Dominated by rooted vegetation—primarily salt-tolerant grasses—that is periodically inundated with the rise and fall of the tide, salt marshes have a complex zonation and structure of plants, animals, and microbes. This biota is tuned to the stresses of salinity fluctuations, alternate drying and submergence, and extreme daily and seasonal temperature variations. Salt marshes are among the most productive ecosystems of the world. A maze of tidal creeks that exhibit fluctuating water levels and carry plankton, fish, and nutrients crisscross the marsh, forming conduits for energy and material exchange with the adjacent estuary.

Sea lavender (Limonium vulgare) growing with glasswort (Salicornia europaea). © Jan van de Kam/Bruce Coleman Ltd.

The salt marsh forms an important interface between terrestrial and marine habitats.

The most common site for a salt marsh, after estuaries and lagoons, is on the sheltered side of a sand or shingle spit. Alongshore currents deposit coarser material on beaches but carry the fine material until it reaches the quieter water behind the barrier. As plants colonize the area, they slow down the flow of water and cause even more silt to accumulate. The Atlantic coast of North America has over 600,000 hectares (2,300 square miles) of salt marshes dominated by the marsh grass *Spartina*.

On the European side of the North Atlantic the flora includes other important components such as the sea pink (*Armeria*), sea lavender (*Limonium*), and sea plantain (*Plantago maritima*). In the course of history large areas of salt marsh in Europe have been used for grazing cattle and sheep, and these areas subsequently have been dominated by the grasses *Puccinella* and *Festuca*. Early colonists in North America often erected dikes around the marshes to keep out the sea; the reclaimed land was used for agriculture in much the same way that it had been in Holland and Belgium.

Only a very small proportion of salt marsh vegetation is eaten directly by animals. The remainder dies, decays, and becomes suspended as fine particles (detritus) in the water. It was thought at one time that the export of this detritus on every ebbing tide supplied large amounts of nutritious food material to the animals in nearby estuarine or coastal waters. Detailed field studies have failed to support this view, and it is now thought that most of the production of salt marsh plants is decomposed by bacteria and fungi and that the plant nutrients are recycled within the marsh. Salt marshes are important habitats for oysters, shrimps, crabs, flatfish, and mullet. They also support

THE RANN OF KACHCHH

The Rann of Kachchh, which is also spelled Kutch, Cutch, or Kachh, is a region of saline mudflats in west-central India and southern Pakistan. The Great Rann covers an area of about 18,000 square km (7,000 square miles) and lies almost entirely within Gujarāt state, India, along the border with Pakistan. The Little Rann of Kachchh extends northeast from the Gulf of Kachchh and occupies about 5,100 square km (2,000 square miles) in Gujarāt state. Originally an extension of the Arabian Sea, the Rann of Kachchh has been closed off by centuries of silting. During the time of Alexander the Great it was a navigable lake, but it is now an extensive mudflat, inundated during monsoon seasons. Settlement is limited to low, isolated hills.

In 1965 a dispute arose over the India-Pakistan boundary line toward the western end of the Great Rann. Fighting broke out in April and ended only when Great Britain intervened to secure a cease-fire. On the report of the United Nations secretary-general to the Security Council, the dispute was referred to an international tribunal, which in 1968 awarded about 10 percent of the border area to Pakistan and about 90 percent to India; the partition was effected in 1969.

large numbers of birds that stop over in the course of migration.

FRESHWATER TIDAL MARSHES

This category includes freshwater marshes close enough to coasts to experience significant tides but far enough upriver in the estuary to be beyond the reach of oceanic salt water. This set of circumstances usually occurs where fresh river water runs to the coast and where the morphology of the coast amplifies the tide as it moves inland. Freshwater tidal marshes are interesting because they receive the same "tidal subsidy" as coastal salt marshes but without the stress of salinity. They act in many ways like salt marshes, but the biota reflect the increased diversity made possible by the reduction of the salt stress found in salt marshes. Plant diversity is high, and more birds use these marshes than any other marsh type. In most parts of the world, the location of freshwater tidal marshes corresponds to sites determined by humans as optimal for habitation and eventual development of cities—i.e., those areas that provide a reliable source of fresh water as well as a physical connection to the sea for ships. Thus freshwater tidal marshes are among the wetland types that have been most altered or destroyed by urban development around the world. Examples of the impact human development has had on wetlands are found in Chesapeake Bay and the lower Delaware River in the eastern United States.

SEAWEED-BASED SYSTEMS

In seaweed-based systems seaweeds vary in size from giant kelps 40 metres (130 feet) or more in length, through the common rockweeds that are 1 or 2 metres (3.28 or 6.56 feet) long, to species that are so small as to be barely visible. They are algae and differ from flowering plants in having a holdfast instead of roots, a stipe instead of a stem, and a blade or thallus instead of leaves. They depend on water movement to continuously provide nutrients, which they take up through the surface of the blade. Kelp is a general term for large brown algae of the order Laminariales. They live predominantly just below low-tide mark and form dense beds reminiscent of underwater forests. They absorb a great deal of wave action, helping to defend shorelines against storms.

The giant kelps that occur along the Pacific coast of the United States and South America have been studied extensively because they are harvested for the extraction of alginates and other substances used in food processing. Typically growing in about 10 metres (32.8

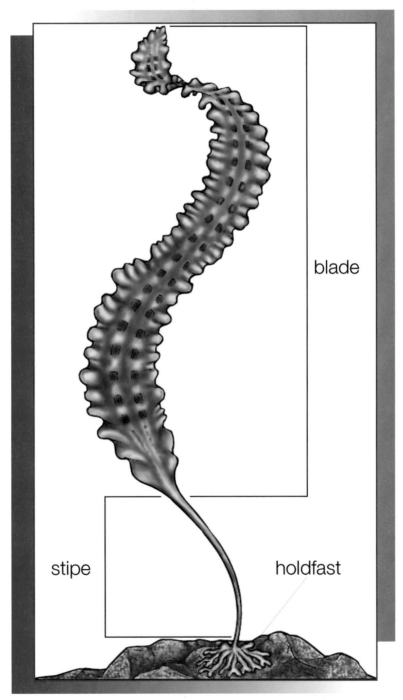

Structure of the kelp Laminaria agardhii. Encyclopaedia Britannica, Inc.

feet) of water, they have large holdfasts from which several stipes originate. A young stipe grows as much as 45 cm (18 inches) per day, reaches the surface of the water, and then trails downstream. A large number of relatively small blades grow from the stipe and form a surface canopy with which they intercept light and nutrients. Giant kelp beds are home to a rich variety of invertebrates and fish, and, in many regions, to the sea otter (*Enhydra lutis*). Sea otters were once abundant around the North Pacific rim from Japan to California, but their range was greatly reduced by hunting. They have recently been reintroduced and populations are growing in many parts of British Columbia in Canada and Washington, Oregon, and California in the United States. Sometimes the sea urchin *Strongylocentrotus* becomes extremely abundant; in the course of feeding on the stipes of the kelps it may destroy kelp beds over large areas. The sea otter is a predator of sea urchins, and where it is abundant it has been shown to control sea urchin numbers. Abalone, a favourite food of sea otters as well as humans, are often abundant in kelp beds.

The characteristic kelps of the North Atlantic are species of *Laminaria* that grow in dense beds but extend only one or two metres (3.28 or 6.56 feet) above the bottom. A characteristic inhabitant of these kelp beds is the Atlantic lobster, *Homarus americanus*, which includes sea urchins in its diet. In the 1970s in Nova Scotia, Can., there was a major outbreak of destructive grazing by sea urchins. This outbreak was accompanied by a sharp decline in lobster populations, suggesting that when lobsters are scarce sea urchin numbers proliferate. However, the question of whether lobsters control sea urchin numbers is still undecided. In the Southern Hemisphere *Macrocystis* and *Laminaria* also occur, but the giant kelp *Lessonia* is important in South America, as is *Ecklonia* in South Africa and Australia.

Rockweed is a general term for the familiar brown seaweeds of the order Fucales, which grow between high- and low-tide marks (the intertidal zone) on rocky shores. In the Northern Hemisphere *Fucus* and *Ascophyllum* are common genera. The latter may be recognized by possession of small air-filled bladders on the fronds. It usually grows in more sheltered locations than *Fucus*. The intertidal zone is of interest because of the zonation of organisms that occurs there. It is in many ways an ideal laboratory in which to study the factors controlling the population size of seaweeds and invertebrates. A high proportion of the animals and algae in this zone are firmly attached to the rocks in order to withstand the force of waves breaking on the shore. Attached fauna include barnacles, limpets, periwinkles, and mussels. Barnacles are crustaceans that are attached to rocks along their backs, with upward-pointing legs that are surrounded by a row of protective hard plates. Limpets are mollusks that live under a very strong conical shell and cling to the rock by an adhesive "foot." Barnacles filter fine particles of seaweed and plankton from the water, while limpets graze on the very small algae growing on the rock surface. Periwinkles are marine snails with hard shells that find shelter among the rockweeds on which they browse. Clamlike mussels are able to anchor themselves firmly to the rocks by means of strong threads; they feed by filtering water. Characteristic predators of these animals are large snails known as whelks, as well as crabs and starfishes. Several kinds of fish enter the rockweed zone at high tide and feed on the invertebrates.

Zonation of seaweeds and animals in the intertidal zone results partly from adaptation to a gradient of physical conditions and partly from competitive interactions between the organisms. The upper part of the intertidal zone is exposed to the air for a longer period and thus is at greater risk of drying out, baking, freezing, or being exposed to rainwater. Algal zonation occurs according to the ability of a species to tolerate these environmental factors, and this in turn influences the type of animal that will inhabit each zone of seaweed. The reverse effect also operates, because by their feeding activity, grazers exclude some seaweeds from zones to which they are otherwise suited.

At the next level in the food web (that of consumers), predators such as starfish control the abundance of grazing animals. In classic experiments on the coast of Washington state, the ecologist Robert Paine demonstrated that removal of the starfish *Pisaster ochraceus* from a section of shoreline caused the community to change from one containing 30 species to one totally dominated by the mussel *Mytilus californianus*. Mussels in this location have the ability to outcompete all other organisms for space on the rocks. Only when the mussel population is controlled by the starfish is a diverse community able to develop. Since these pioneering studies were carried out, many comparable effects have been demonstrated elsewhere. For example, in some places, barnacles are competitive dominants, but their abundance is controlled by limpets and whelks.

SEA-GRASS BEDS

Sea-grass beds are found just below low-tide mark in all latitudes. In north temperate waters *Zostera* is the most common genus, while in tropical climates *Thalassia*, known as turtle grass, is an important element. As with marsh grasses, it seems that most of the plant material produced is decomposed by fungi and bacteria while the nutrients are recycled. The sea-grass beds slow the flow of water, causing deposition of silt in which worms and clams may burrow. The plants present a large surface area on which small algae grow, providing a nutritious source of food for browsing animals. The sea-grass beds also shelter many small organisms from their predators, and various species of fish lay their eggs close to sea-grass beds so that the young fish can take advantage of this shelter. Manatees and dugongs, often known as sea cows, are marine mammals that specialize in feeding on sea grasses. This was once a diverse and abundant group, but there are now only three species of manatee (genus *Trichecus*) and one dugong species (*Dugong dugon*). The manatees inhabit the eastern and western shores of the Atlantic, while dugongs are found from East Africa to Southeast Asia and Australia. They reach two to three metres (6.56 or 9.84 feet) in length and feed by ploughing along the bottom, ingesting rhizomes, stems, and leaves of sea grass. Dugongs in northern Australia can occur in herds of 100 to 200 and need very large areas of sea-grass beds to support them. Green turtles (*Chelonia midas*), which compete with dugongs for sea grass as food, occur throughout the tropics and are much more abundant than dugongs. In the area of the Great Barrier Reef, nesting colonies of green turtles have been observed that contain between 11,000 and 12,000 individuals.

BEACHES AND MUDFLATS

Large areas of coastal habitat have sediments that are too unstable to support communities of large plants. They often have populations of microscopic algae growing at the surface, and they receive particles of decomposing organic matter derived from nearby seaweed or sea-grass beds. A beach near the high-tide level may be so unstable that few animals are able to live in it, but a little farther out to sea the mudflats or sand flats support a rich community of burrowing animals such as polychaete worms, clams, and burrowing shrimps. Many of the worms ingest the sediment and derive nourishment from the organic matter contained in it. Others have tubes that reach to the surface so that they can filter food particles from the water when they are covered by the tide. Clams usually feed in the same way. Crustaceans, starfish, and various kinds of finfish, especially flatfish, move over the mudflats at high tide in search of prey. Mudflats and sand flats are important feeding grounds for wading birds such as sandpipers, oystercatchers, and plovers. In temperate climates such birds may remain year-round, but many hundreds of thousands of birds make seasonal migrations between high-latitude summer habitats and low-latitude wintering grounds. Large flocks rely on intertidal flats for feeding along the way. For example, it has been shown that about 70,000 semipalmated sandpipers stop on the mudflats of the upper Bay of Fundy, in eastern Canada, in July and August of each year. Feeding predominantly on the burrowing amphipod shrimp *Corophium volutator*, each bird takes 10,000 to 20,000 shrimps and accumulates 13 to 18 grams (0.46 to 0.63 ounce) of fat, comprising one-third to one-half of the body weight, before taking off on a nonstop journey to the Lesser Antilles or the north coast of South America. At one time there was a plan to build a dam for tidal power that would have permanently flooded these tidal flats, and this would have been a disastrous loss of habitat for these migratory birds.

INLAND WETLAND SYSTEMS

Inland wetland systems span freshwater marshes, bogs, forested swamps, and riparian ecosystems. Inland systems are typically characterized by the periodic influx of freshwater from precipitation or runoff from upstream areas, and they support biological communities that are largely dependent on freshwater environments.

FRESHWATER MARSHES

The wetlands in this diverse group are unified primarily by the fact that they are all nontidal freshwater systems dominated by grasses, sedges, and other freshwater hydrophytes. However, they differ in their geologic origins and their driving hydrologic forces, and they vary in size from small pothole marshes less than a hectare in size to the immense saw grass monocultures of the Florida Everglades. Vegetation is dominated by graminoids and sedges such as the tall reeds *Typha* (cattails) and *Phragmites*, the grasses *Panicum* and *Cladium*, the sedges *Cyperus* and *Carex*, and floating aquatic plants such as *Nymphaea* and *Nelumbo* in temperate regions and *Eichhornia crassipes* in tropical and subtropical climes. Some inland marshes, such as the prairie glacial marshes of North America, follow a 5- to 20-year cycle of drought. During this period the marsh dries out and exposes large areas of mudflat upon which dense seedling stands germinate. When the rains return, flooding drowns the annual seedlings while allowing the perennials to spread rapidly and vigorously. Deterioration of the marsh follows and is sometimes associated with concentrated muskrat activity. The cycle then repeats.

The substrate of inland marshes has a higher pH and a greater availability of minerals than does the substrate of bogs. Freshwater marshes are often very productive ecosystems, and most of that productivity is routed through detrital pathways. Herbivory can be important, particularly by muskrats and geese, and consumers can have very significant effects on ecosystem development.

PANTANAL

The Pantanal is a floodplain in south-central Brazil that extends into northeast Paraguay and southeast Bolivia. It lies mainly within the Brazilian *estados* (states) of Mato Grosso do Sul and Mato Grosso. The Pantanal is one of the world's largest freshwater wetlands, and the extent of its dynamic area is estimated to be from 140,000 square km (54,000 square miles) to 210,000 square km (81,000 square miles). The wetlands extend for about 600 km (375 miles) north-to-south along the banks of the upper Paraguay River and several of its tributaries, including the São Lourenço and the Taquari rivers.

The Pantanal is a gigantic seasonal floodplain. During the summer rainy season (November–March), the rivers overflow their banks and flood the adjacent lowlands, forming shallow lakes and innumerable swamps and marshes and leaving islandlike areas of higher ground. During the drier winter season (April–September), the rivers withdraw into their banks, but the lowlands are only partially drained. The sediments carried by the floods confer great fertility on the Pantanal's soils, which support scattered trees, rushes, and grasses and a rich assortment of wildlife consisting of more than 600 species of birds, 200 species of fishes, and many mammals and reptiles. The Pantanal's grazing lands have supported cattle raising, but by the late 20th century the activities of gold miners and farmers in surrounding areas, and the effects of poachers and tourists in the Pantanal itself, threatened to upset the wetlands' delicate ecology.

BOGS AND FENS

Bogs and fens belong to a major class of wetlands called peatlands, moors, or mires, which occur throughout much of the boreal zone of the world. Bogs and fens are distributed in cold temperate climates, mostly in the Northern Hemisphere. There, ample precipitation and high humidity from maritime influences, combined with low evapotranspiration, lead to moisture accumulation. Bogs are acid peat deposits that generally have a high water table (the upper surface of groundwater) but no significant inflow or outflow of streams. Because of their low pH, they support acidophilic (acid-loving) vegetation, particularly mosses. Fens are open wetland systems that generally receive some drainage from surrounding mineral soils and are often covered by grasses, sedges, or reeds. Extensive areas of bogs and fens occur in Finland, eastern Europe, western Siberia, Alaska, Canada (especially Labrador), and the north-central United States. Canada has approximately 1.3 million square km (502,000 square miles) of peatlands, making it the largest resource for peat in the world. In the United States, bogs and fens usually develop in basins scoured out by the Pleistocene glaciers and are clustered primarily around the Great Lakes region and in Maine.

PEAT AND PEAT MOSS

Compression and chemical breakdown of dead plants and other vegetable debris cause formation of the organic substance known as peat, which is harvested and dried for use as fuel.

An organic fuel consisting of spongy material formed by the par-

Peat moss (Sphagnum flexuosum). K.G. Preston-Mafham/The Natural History Photographic Agency

tial decomposition of organic matter, primarily plant material, in wetlands such as swamps, muskegs, bogs, fens, and moors. The development of peat is favoured by warm, moist climatic conditions; however, peat can develop even in cold regions such as Siberia, Canada, and Scandinavia. Peat is only a minor contributor to the world energy supply, but large deposits occur in Canada, China, Indonesia, Russia, Scandinavia, and the United States. Major users include Finland, Ireland, Russia, and Sweden.

The formation of peat is the first step in the formation of coal. With increasing depth of burial and increasing temperature, peat deposits are gradually changed to lignite. With increased time and higher temperatures, these low-rank coals are gradually converted to subbituminous and bituminous coal and under certain conditions to anthracite.

Dried peat burns readily with a smoky flame and a characteristic odour. The ash is powdery and light, except for varieties that have a high content of inorganic matter. Peat is used for domestic heating purposes and forms a fuel suitable for boiler firing in either briquetted or pulverized form. It also has been used to produce electricity.

Peat moss, which is also called bog moss or sphagnum moss, includes any of more than 150–300 species of plants in the subclass Sphagnidae, of the division Bryophyta, comprising the family Sphagnaceae, which contains one genus, *Sphagnum*. The taxonomy of Sphagnum species remains controversial, with various botanists accepting quite different numbers of species. The pale green to deep red plants, up to 30 cm (about 12 inches) tall, form dense clumps around ponds, in swamps and bogs, on moist, acid cliffs, and on lakeshores from tropical to subpolar regions. The veinless leaves and stem cortex contain many interconnected, enlarged dead cells, with external openings through which water can enter; the plants hold up to 20 times their weight in water.

Each spherical brown sporangium, or spore case, shrinks as it dries, creating internal pressure that casts off the lid (operculum) and shoots the spores as far as 10 cm (4 inches) from the plant. The metabolic processes of growing peat moss cause an increase in the acidity of the surrounding water, thus reducing bacterial action and preventing decay. Peat moss forms several types of bogs in northern areas.

Dried peat moss has been used for surgical dressings, diapers, lamp wicks, bedding, and stable litter. It is commonly employed as a packing material by florists and shippers of live aquatic animals and as a seedbed cover and soil additive by gardeners, who value its ability to increase soil moisture, porosity, and acidity. Peat mosses are valuable in erosion control, and properly drained peat bogs provide useful agricultural land.

FORESTED SWAMPS

The term "swamp" usually refers to a wetlands system dominated by trees or other woody vegetation. A wide variety of such systems are found throughout the world. In the tropics vast swamps (which are also called riparian systems) are found along the great rivers, by which they are often inundated for many months. In temperate regions forested swamps can be dominated by trees that tolerate permanent to semipermanent flooding such as the bald cypress (*Taxodium*) or swamp tupelo (*Nyssa*) in the southern United States or the alder (*Alnus*) or maple (*Acer*) in more temperate climes.

RIPARIAN SYSTEMS

Riparian systems occur along rivers and streams that periodically crest their channel confines, causing flooding. They are also in evidence in places in which a meandering channel creates new sites for plant life to take root and grow. The soils and amount of moisture they contain are influenced by the adjacent stream or river. These systems are distinguished by their linear form and by large fluxes of energy and materials delivered by upstream systems. In arid regions riparian systems can exist along or in ephemeral streams and on the floodplains of perennial streams. In most nonarid regions riparian zones usually develop first along the region of the stream where water flow is constant—i.e., the point at which sufficient groundwater enters the channel to sustain flow through dry periods. Riparian ecosystems exist as broad, alluvial valleys several tens of kilometres wide, as in the Amazon Basin in South America and in Bangladesh, or they can be narrow strips of vegetation along the bank of a stream, as is often seen in the arid western United States. The riparian zone is valuable to animals as a refuge, as an abundant source of water, and as a corridor for migration. This is particularly true in arid regions, where riparian zones may support the only significant vegetation in many kilometres.

WETLAND MANAGEMENT

Among ecosystems that are easiest to destroy permanently are these boundary ecosystems. Wetlands can be isolated from their hydrologic source and essentially destroyed if drainage areas are altered or impoundments are built. Major cities in the United States such as Chicago and Washington, D.C., stand on sites that were, in part, wetlands. The amount of wetlands lost worldwide is almost impossible to determine. However, it is known that in the lower 48 states of the United States, a relatively newly developed region of the world, more than half of the original wetlands have been lost, primarily to agricultural development.

Humans have been utilizing wetlands for centuries. Early civilizations, such as the ancient Babylonians, the Egyptians, and the Aztec, developed unique systems of water delivery that involved wetlands. Among the peoples currently living in proximity to wetlands (known as "wetlanders") whose culture is linked to these systems are the Camarguais of southern France, the Cajuns of Louisiana, and the Ma'dan, or Marsh Arabs, of southern Iraq; after hundreds of years, all still live in harmony with wetlands. Countless plant and animal products are harvested from wetlands in countries such as China. A thriving modern industry continues to depend on the harvest of cranberries from bogs in the United States. The Russians and the Irish have mined their peatlands for several centuries as a source of energy. Many countries throughout South and Southeast Asia, East Africa, and Central and South America depend on mangrove wetlands for timber, food, and tannin. For centuries salt marshes in northern Europe and the British Isles, and later in New England, have been used to graze animals and raise crops of hay. Thatch roofs and fences have been built from materials retrieved from these areas. Reeds from the wetlands of Romania, Iraq, Japan, and China are used for similar purposes. Techniques to produce fish in systems integrated into rice paddies or shallow ponds were developed several thousand years ago in China and Southeast Asia; crayfish harvesting is still practiced in the wetlands of Louisiana and the Philippines.

Recognition of the importance of wetlands is growing, with the result that many are being protected by local and national policies (particularly in the United States) as well as by international projects. Examples of these efforts include the Ramsar Convention, which is an international agreement set up for the protection of habitat for migratory waterfowl and other avian life, and the North American Waterfowl Management Plan. Wetland recognition and protection is becoming one of the most important facets of global natural resource protection.

WETLAND ECOLOGY

Combining the attributes of both aquatic and terrestrial ecosystems, but falling outside each category, wetlands inhabit a space betwixt and between the disciplines of terrestrial and aquatic ecology. Consequently, their unique properties are not adequately addressed by present ecological paradigms. With their unique characteristics of standing water or waterlogged soils, anoxic conditions, and plant and animal adaptations, wetlands serve as testing grounds for "universal" ecological theories and principles such as succession and energy flow, concepts developed primarily with aquatic or terrestrial ecosystems in mind. These boundary ecosystems also provide an excellent laboratory for the study of principles related to transition zones, ecological interfaces, and ecotones. In order for wetlands to be protected or restored in the best possible manner, a multidisciplinary approach to their study is required.

CHAPTER 6
WETLAND FLORA AND FAUNA

Wetland biota is largely the product of the chemical conditions of the surrounding waters. Saltwater plants must possess features that allow them to adapt to highly saline conditions, and many freshwater wetland plants possess adaptations to deal with challenges ranging from soils that are temporarily waterlogged to flooding episodes that fully submerge the plant. In addition, many aquatic animals possess features or behaviours that allow them to deal with the chemical challenges posed by the water they live in. Animal diversity in swamps, however, is largely a function of plant diversity rather than the chemical conditions of the water.

BOG BIOTA

Typical bogs have simple floras, including moss, *Sphagnums*, and heaths. *Sphagnums* are large mosses with large empty cells with pores opening to the outside that lie between the chlorophyll-bearing cells of the leaves. These empty cells readily absorb and retain water, giving a spongelike quality to the moss. *Sphagnum* absorbs minerals (cations) from the water, replacing them with acid (hydrogen ions), and thus makes the water around itself more acid. Other than *Sphagnums* and heaths, there are a few sedges and grasses, such as cotton grass; insectivorous sundews; pitcher plants; and many orchids. Desmids, a group of unicellular green algae divided into symmetrical halves, are characteristic of bogs. Animals are not common on bogs.

The plants of raised bogs are mainly broad-leaved evergreen trees, which may be as tall as 30 metres (100 feet). Palms and screwpines may also occur. The number

HEATHS

Heaths are any of the low evergreen shrubs of the genus *Erica* belonging to the family Ericaceae. Ericaceae is made up of about 500 species, most of which are indigenous to South Africa, where they are especially diverse in the southwestern Cape region. Some heaths also occur in the Mediterranean region and in northern Europe, and species have been introduced to North America.

The heaths have small, usually very narrow leaves arranged in whorls set closely together on the shoots. The long-lasting flowers have four sepals, a four-cleft, bell-shaped, or tubular corolla (ring of petals), inflated in many species, and a four-celled capsule. Most heaths are low shrubs, but some African species are large bushes or trees. Pollination of the flowers may be by wind, birds, or insects depending on the species. Although most species have dry fruits that open to release the small seeds, a few have fleshy fruits.

The purple, or Scotch, heath, or bell heather (*E. cinerea*), is common in Great Britain and western Europe; its minute flowers yield much nectar. Other British species are cross-leaved heath, or bog heather (*E. tetralix*); Cornish heath (*E. vagans*), found also in western Europe; fringed heath (*E. ciliaris*), in western England and Ireland; and Irish heath (*E. mediterranea*), which reaches 1 to 1.5 metres (3 to 5 feet) tall in Ireland. The white, or tree, heath (*E. arborea*), found in southern France and the Mediterranean region, is the source of briar root, used for mak-

Heath (Erica carnea). Douglas David Dawn

ing briarwood pipes. Some southern African species (e.g., *E. melanthera, E. verticillata,* and *E. ventricosa*) are cultivated in cool greenhouses and outdoors in southwestern North America.

of kinds of plants of these bogs is very limited in comparison with the surrounding forests, just as is the case in colder bogs. Toward the centre of the raised bogs, trees are shorter or absent. Grasses and sedges cover more of the ground and open pools of water may occur. *Sphagnum* does not grow in tropical bogs to any extent, and the peat is composed of the remains of seed plants. The limited number of species is caused entirely by the lack of any groundwater supply of minerals and the rapid removal, by heavy rainfall, of those that arrive in dust.

MARSH FLORA

The number of plant species in marshes is few compared to the numbers that grow on well-watered but not water-logged land. Grasses, grasslike sedges, and reeds or rushes are of major importance.

One of the more dominant groups of marsh grasses is cordgrass, which is also called salt grass or simply marsh grass. Cordgrass is made up of any of 16 species of grasses constituting the genus *Spartina* (family Poaceae). The erect, tough, long-leaved plants range from 0.3 to 3 metres (1 to 10 feet) in height and are found on marshes and tidal mud flats of North America, Europe, and Africa.

Most species grow in clumps, with short flower spikes alternating along and often adherent to the upper portion of the stems, and with spreading underground stems (rhizomes) that send up new plants and are good soil binders. Prairie cordgrass (*Spartina pectinata*) and gulf cordgrass (*S. spartinae*) are the most widely distributed North American species.

Wild rice is of some commercial importance, but true rice is undoubtedly by far the most important marsh plant and supplies a major portion of the world's grain.

Saltmeadow cordgrass (Spartina patens). Grant Heilman Photography

ANIMALS OF THE MARSH

Animals have adapted to the limited supplies of oxygen in salt-marsh water in various ways. Rat-tailed maggots (*Tubifera*), for example, survive in shallow marshes by means of a telescoping, tail-breathing tube that they extend to the water surface for air. Some larvae of shore flies (Ephydridae) and some nematodes take advantage of the air spaces in plants and obtain oxygen from that source. Many small marsh animals have great resistance to lack of oxygen; for example, many nematodes can live indefinitely in the complete absence of oxygen. This ability is essential for such minute animals that would otherwise be limited in distribution to a thin layer a fraction of an inch deep at the mud surface.

Salt-marsh animals living at or in the ground are largely derived from marine ancestors and have a problem in resisting fresh water from rains rather than salt. Some, such as worms, merely hide in the mud until the freshwater has run off the marsh surface. Others, such as fiddler crabs, have developed the ability to control their osmotic concentration in freshwater for periods of up to several days. Insects are the principal land animals found on marshes. Although they can withstand short periods of saltwater immersion, they often avoid saltwater by moving up the plants or flying away.

TREES AND OTHER PLANTS OF THE SWAMP

The number of plant species in swamps is few compared to the numbers that grow on well-watered but not waterlogged land. Cattails (*Typha*) and common reeds (*Phragmites*) are familiar swamp species around the world. Papyrus, a sedge, is widespread in the tropics. Bald cypress is an example of a tree adapted to growth in swamps, but gums, willows, alders, and maples are also common.

Tropical swamps have many tree species including palms. Tropical swamp trees often develop buttresses that apparently help support them, though buttresses are also common on many upland trees in the tropics. Generally, all swamp trees lack deep-growing roots. Roots tend to stay near the surface, probably because of the lack of oxygen in the soil. Being near the surface gives a large lateral spread to the root system, which also gives the tree support against lateral stresses from winds or water flow. The shallowness of the roots also often produces the appearance of buttresses in temperate swamp trees because the beginnings of the roots, usually hidden in the soil, are visible at the surface.

Different species of trees that grow in temporary swamps differ considerably in their resistance to submersion—i.e., to lack of oxygen. This is serious during the submersion period but is not a problem in drier periods, at least in the shallow layers of the soil. In North American swamps, alders and willows will survive or even thrive on land immersed for periods as long as one month, whereas red gum survives only about two weeks. Cottonwood begins to show the effects of submergence after only two days and survives only one week.

SALT SWAMP FLORA

Salt swamps are formed by seawater flooding and draining, which exposes flat areas of intertidal land. Regularly flooded, protected areas develop mangrove swamps in tropical and subtropical regions. Mangroves will grow in pure sand at the edge of the sea.

Mangroves (Rhizophora apiculata) at low tide on the coast of Thailand. C.B. Frith/Bruce Coleman Inc.

Mangroves are made up of certain shrubs and trees that belong primarily to the families Rhizophoraceae, Acanthaceae, Lythraceae, Combretaceae, and Arecaceae (Palmae), that grow in dense thickets or forests along tidal estuaries, in salt marshes, and on muddy coasts, and that characteristically have prop roots—i.e., exposed, supporting roots. The term *mangrove* also applies to thickets and forests of such plants. Respiratory or knee roots (pneumatophores) are characteristic of many species; they project above the mud and have small openings (lenticels) through which air enters, passing through the soft, spongy tissue to the roots beneath the mud.

Mangrove flora along the Atlantic coast of tropical America and along the coast of the Gulf of Mexico to Florida consists chiefly of the common, or red, mangrove (*Rhizophora mangle*) of the family Rhizophoraceae

Red mangroves in Oyster Bay, Everglades National Park. Tim Kiusalaas/ Photographer's Choice/Getty Images

and the black mangrove (*Avicennia nitida,* sometimes *A. marina*) of the family Acanthaceae. Mangrove formations in Southeast Asia include *Sonneratia* of the family Lythraceae and the nipa palm (*Nypa fruticans*) of the family Arecaceae.

The trunks and branches of the common mangrove are typical of the growth habit of all mangroves. They constantly produce adventitious roots, which, descending in arched fashion, strike at some distance from the parent stem and send up new trunks. While the fruit is still attached to the parent branch, the long embryonic root emerges from the seed and grows rapidly downward. When the seed falls, the young root is in the correct position to be driven into the mud; the plant being thus rooted, the shoot makes its appearance. The young root may grow to such a length that it becomes fixed in the mud before the fruit separates from the parent tree.

Common mangrove (Rhizophora mangle). Grant Heilman Photography

The common mangrove grows to about 9 metres (30 feet) tall. The leaves are 5 to 15 cm (2 to 6 inches) long, opposite, oval or elliptic, and smooth-edged; they are thick, have leathery surfaces, and are borne on short stems. The flowers are pale yellow.

The black mangrove, usually of moderate height, sometimes grows 18 to 21 metres (60 to 70 feet) tall. The leaves are 5 to 7.5 cm (2 to 3 inches) long, opposite, oblong or spear-shaped; the upper surface is green and glossy, the lower surface whitish or grayish. The white flowers are small, inconspicuous, and fragrant and are frequented by honeybees for their abundant nectar.

The wood of some species is hard and durable. The astringent bark yields a water-soluble tanning substance. The fruit of the common mangrove is sweet and wholesome.

SWAMP FAUNA

The tops of mangrove trees shelter a diverse group of animals that are unaffected by seawater, because they never make contact with it. In general, swamp animals are little affected by wetland conditions except as those conditions affect the species of trees growing in the swamp. Whereas the diversity of plants is limited by the stresses that the presence of water entails, the animal diversity is more a reflection of the plant diversity than the nature of the water supply.

SPECIFIC WETLAND REGIONS

Several large wetland areas of note dot Earth's surface. Most are extensions of the freshwater lakes and rivers that feed them. However, one, the Sundarbans of India and Bangladesh, is primarily a network of saltwater estuaries.

BANGWEULU

Bangweulu (Bantu: "Large Water") is a shallow lake with extensive swamps in northeastern Zambia. It is part of the Congo River system. Lying at an elevation of 1,140 metres (3,740 feet), the waters of Bangweulu, fluctuating with the rainy season, cover a triangular area of about 9,800 square km (3,800 square miles). The lake, at the triangle's northwest corner, is 72 km (45 miles) long and 38 km (24 miles) wide. There are three inhabited islands in the lake and many low islands in the swamps. The swamplands are the result of excessive vegetation growth over a section of low gradient along the course of the Chambeshi River, where they act as a check to the annual flooding, releasing the floodwaters slowly through a myriad of channels and lagoons, to issue as the Luapula River where the slope increases again. The vegetation responsible for the swamps consists of a common water reed, *Phragmites communis,* growing just above mean water level; a zone of papyrus at water level; and a floating grass, called hippo-grass, in deeper water. The lake's fish are caught, dried, and exported to the copper-mining belt 160 km (100 miles) to the west. The explorer-missionary Dr. David Livingstone, the first European to visit the lake (1868), died on its southern shore in 1873.

BIG CYPRESS SWAMP

Big Cypress Swamp is a large forest morass lying mainly in Collier county, southern Florida, U.S., and covering 6,200 square km (2,400 square miles). The region merges into the swampy Everglades to the east and south. It is dominated by cypress trees, and wildlife is abundant. Sunniland, a village in the swamp about 65 km (40 miles) southeast of Fort Myers, was the site of the first oil wells in Florida. The Seminole and Miccosukee Indians have reservations in the area, which is crossed west to east by the Everglades Parkway.

Big Cypress National Preserve, established in 1974, covers some 3,100 square km (1,200 square miles) on the swamp's eastern half. It was created because of the importance of its watershed to Everglades National Park, which borders it on the south. The preserve provides habitat for such endangered species as the Florida cougar (*Felis concolor coryi*).

CONGAREE NATIONAL PARK

Congaree National Park is a natural area in central South Carolina, U.S., about 30 km (20 miles) southeast of Columbia. Authorized in 1976 as Congaree Swamp National Monument, it was designated a national park and renamed in 2003; it became an international biosphere reserve in 1981. The park has an area of 90 square km (35 square miles).

Congaree Swamp, the focus of the national park, is the largest area of virgin Southern bottomland hardwoods remaining in the United States. The park consists of an alluvial floodplain on the meandering Congaree River. Flooding occurs about 10 times a year but lasts only from several days to a month at a time, and for most of the year the area is dry. The tract includes loblolly pine, sweet gum, water tupelo, bald cypress, hickory, and oak—some of record size—and also rare and endangered species of both plants and animals, such as the red-cockaded woodpecker. Deer, opossums, foxes, feral swine, and bobcats are found in the swamp forest. Access to the park is by trail or boat; canoeing is a popular activity.

Congaree National Park, South Carolina, U.S. Robert C. Clark/Stock Option

THE EVERGLADES

The Everglades is a subtropical saw-grass marsh region up to 80 km (50 miles) wide but generally less than 0.3 metre (1 foot) deep, covering more than 11,100 square km (4,300 square miles) of southern Florida, U.S. Water in this "river of grass" moves slowly southward to mangrove swamps bordering the Gulf of Mexico to the southwest and Florida Bay to the south. To the east the marsh reaches near the narrow, sandy belt that includes the Miami metropolitan area, and to the west it merges into Big Cypress Swamp. The name Everglades is a term unique to Florida. *Glade* has been used to refer to an open, grassy area in the forest or a moist, swampy area; *ever* may have referred to the marsh's seemingly interminable expanse.

The Everglades occupies a shallow limestone-floored basin that slopes imperceptibly southward at about about

4 cm per km (2.4 inches per mile). Much of it is covered with saw grass (a sedge, the edges of which are covered with minute sharp teeth), which grows to a height of 1.2 to 3 metres (4 to 10 feet). Open water is sometimes found. Slight changes in the elevation of the land and the water's salt content create different habitats. The Florida Bay estuary is covered with sea grass and serves as a nursery for fish. Mangroves also serve as nurseries and as feeding grounds for wading birds in tidal areas where fresh and salt water combine. Coastal prairie regions support salt-tolerant succulents and cordgrass. Hardwood hammocks consist of thick stands of tropical (mahogany, cocoplum, and strangler fig) and temperate (saw palmetto, live oak, and red maple) trees growing on slight hills, creating islands in the saw-grass marsh and sloughs; domes of cypress or willow can also be found. Pinelands, dominated by slash pine, occupy dry ridges.

The organic soils, formed from the decay of lush vegetation, range from discontinuous shallow patches to accumulations of peat and muck 2.4 to 3 metres (8 to 10 feet) thick near Lake Okeechobee. The best soils are deep mucks found in a narrow zone along the lakeshore, where a dense tangle of custard apple, or pond apple, once grew.

The climate of the Everglades is tropical to subtropical and is influenced strongly by the southeast trade winds. Monthly mean temperatures range from 17 °C (63 °F) to 28 °C (82 °F), though winter frosts occur on rare occasions. Rainfall averages 1,000 to 1,650 mm (40 to 65 inches) annually, with most coming between May and October. During that period the land is nearly covered with a sheet of water. In the dry season (December–April), however, water levels drop and leave it dotted with small pools.

The marsh provides habitat for more than 350 bird species. There are wading birds such as egrets, herons, roseate spoonbills, and ibis; shore and water birds such as

Everglades National Park in Florida. National Park Service

terns, plovers, rails, and sandpipers; birds of prey including owls, hawks, and osprey; and a wide variety of songbirds. Several game fish species make their homes there. The Everglades is known for its population of alligators; bobcats, white-tailed deer, river otters, gray foxes, and many types of snakes, lizards, and turtles also live there. The area provides habitat for endangered species such as the manatee, Florida panther, wood stork, American crocodile, and several species of sea turtle. The population of wading birds in the Everglades has fallen drastically since the mid-20th century.

GREAT DISMAL SWAMP

The Great Dismal Swamp, which is also called Dismal Swamp, is a marshy region on the Coastal Plain of southeastern Virginia and northeastern North Carolina, U.S., between Norfolk, Virginia, and Elizabeth City, North

Carolina. It is densely forested and contains scattered natural elevations of 3 to 6 metres (10 to 20 feet) above sea level. Along the western margin the Pamlico Formation (known as the Great Dismal Swamp Terrace) rises to 7.5 metres (25 feet) and more, forming a natural boundary.

The name Great Dismal was given by Colonel William Byrd of Virginia, who surveyed the region in 1728. In 1763 George Washington, as a member of a surveying and engineering company, surveyed the area with a view to canalizing, draining, and reclaiming it. At that time the swamp was about 65 km (40 miles) long and covered about 5,200 square km (2,000 square miles). In the late 18th century some 160 square km (62 square miles) were drained. The swamp is now about 60 km (37 miles) long north to south and covers an area of approximately 1,940 square km (750 square miles). About 433 square km (167 square miles) of this is protected within Great Dismal Swamp National Wildlife Refuge, established in 1974. Despite much lumbering and widespread destruction of timber by fire, the area is still heavily wooded with cypress, black gum, juniper, and water ash, and a tangle of honeysuckle and woodbine. The swamp was once the habitat of many rare birds, including the ivory-billed woodpecker. The cottonmouth and other poisonous snakes are numerous. The area is noted for fishing and hunting; deer, bears, raccoons, and opossums are plentiful, especially in the nearly inaccessible Coldwater Ditch area.

The Dismal Swamp Canal (built 1790–1828) is an intracoastal waterway 35 km (22 miles) long connecting Chesapeake Bay, by way of Deep Creek and the southern branch of the Elizabeth River, with Albemarle Sound in North Carolina through the Pasquotank River. The canal forms a link in the Atlantic Intracoastal Waterway. In the midst of the swamp is the freshwater Lake Drummond

Lake Drummond in the centre of Great Dismal Swamp, Virginia. Courtesy of the Virginia Department of Conservation and Economic Development

(about 5 km [3 miles] in diameter), which is connected with the canal by the 3-mile-long Feeder Ditch; this lake is the basis of the poem *The Lake of the Dismal Swamp* by the Irish poet Thomas Moore.

HIMMERLAND

The Himmerland is a region of Jutland between Hobro and Ålborg, forming the northernmost non-insular part of Denmark. It is nearly surrounded by water. At Års, the main town of the interior, the Vesthimmerlands Museum displays prehistoric and folk artifacts. Himmerland is a predominantly rural region of villages and farms. Although much of the former wetland has been drained, the leached soils are not highly fertile, and peat bogs still occur in the east. Himmerland's wet, sandy environment supports unusual wildlife species. Eagles live in the 88-square-km (34-square-mile) Lille Vildmose (marsh). Rare clovers, orchids, and blue anemones grow in the Rold Forest, the remnant of a spruce forest that once covered most of the region. North of Rold Forest the heather-covered Rebild Hills, bought by Danish Americans in 1911 and donated to Denmark (1912) as a national park, are the site of annual Danish-American July 4th celebrations

LAKE ḤAMMĀR

Lake Ḥammār (Arabic: Hawr Al-ḥammār) is a large swampy lake in southeastern Iraq, south of the junction of the Tigris and Euphrates rivers. Fed by distributaries of the Euphrates, the lake (110 km [70 miles] long; 1,950 square km [750 square miles] in area) drains via a short channel into the Shatt al-Arab near Basra. It was once only a reed-filled marshland but was later utilized as a natural irrigation reservoir for the fertile soils of the delta region, where dates, rice, and cotton were grown. The lake and surrounding marshlands are the traditional home of the Ma'dan, a tribe of seminomadic marsh dwellers who are sometimes referred to as Marsh Arabs. Their distinctive culture is based on the herding of water buffalo, the hunting of wildfowl and pigs from reed canoes, and the building of elaborate houses of woven reeds (Arabic: *mudhīf*). The structures have

Gothic-appearing arches made of bundles of reeds fastened together at the top; the walls are woven in intricate patterns of reeds. A 4th-millennium-BCE plaque from the Sumerian city of Uruk on the western edge of the marshes depicts such a structure, showing the longevity of the style.

In 1992 the Iraqi government began draining the country's southern marshlands in an attempt to drive out Shī'ite guerrillas who had taken refuge there. By 1993 one-third of Lake Ḥammār was dry and many thousands of the marshlands' residents had moved deeper into the marshes or fled to Iran.

OKAVANGO DELTA

The marshes of the Okavango delta, which lie east of the Kalahari desert in Botswana, are perhaps the best example of marshes formed in an interior, closed basin that has no drainage. The movement of water through the marshes of the Okavango delta is complex and imperfectly understood. The perennial Okavango River runs southward into its delta across the Caprivi Strip from the highlands of Angola. Most of its water evaporates from the 10,000 square km (4,000 square miles) of the delta wetlands. Floodwater reaches down through the eastern side of the marshes to the Boteti River, which flows sporadically to Lake Xau (Dow) and the Makgadikgadi Pans (also roughly 10,000 square km in area). Less and less water flowed through the western side of the Okavango marshes during the 20th century, so that the 180-square-km (70-square-mile) Lake Ngami—famous a century ago—is today dry and almost unrecognizable as a lake. Meanwhile, the eastern Makgadikgadi Pans are flooded annually by the otherwise ephemeral Nata River from the Zimbabwe highlands, while the southern tributaries of the pans are now dry fossil valleys.

The Molopo River and its Ramatlhabama tributary, on the southern border of Botswana with a course flowing into the Orange River, today rarely flood more than 80 km (50 miles) from their sources. Most rivers in Botswana are ephemeral channels, usually not flowing aboveground except in the summer rainy season. The two great exceptions to this rule are vigorous channels fed by the rains of central Africa—the Okavango River above its delta and the Chobe River flowing through its marshes along the northern border to join the Zambezi above the Victoria Falls.

OKEFENOKEE SWAMP

The Okefenokee Swamp is a swamp and wildlife refuge in southeastern Georgia and northern Florida, U.S. It is a shallow, saucer-shaped depression approximately 40 km (25 miles) wide and 65 km (40 miles) long and covers an area of more than 1,550 square km (600 square miles). Lying about 80 km (50 miles) inland from the Atlantic coast, the Okefenokee Swamp is bounded on the east by the low, sandy Trail Ridge, which prevents direct drainage into the Atlantic. The swamp is partially drained southward into the Atlantic by the Suwannee and St. Mary's rivers.

The Okefenokee Swamp includes low, sandy ridges, wet, grassy savannas, small islands (called hummocks) surrounded by marshes, and extensive "prairies," or dark water areas covered by undergrowth and trees. Vegetation is dense in the swamp and includes giant tupelo and bald cypress trees festooned with Spanish moss, brush, and vines; where sandy soil is above the water, pine trees predominate. Meandering channels of open water form an intricate maze. Exotic flowers, among them floating hearts, lilies, and rare orchids, abound. The swamp is populated with diverse and abundant wildlife, with about 175 species of birds and at least 40 species of mammals, which include raccoons, black bear, white-tailed deer, bobcats, fox, and otter. Alligators are also present.

In 1937, 150,319 hectares (371,445 acres) of swampland, almost all in Georgia, were set aside as the Okefenokee National Wildlife Refuge, with headquarters at Waycross, Ga. The swamp's name probably is derived from the Seminole Indian word for "trembling earth," so-called because of the floating islands of the swamp.

PRIPET MARSHES

The Pripet Marshes (Ukrainian: Polissya; Belarusian: Palyessye; Polish: Polesie, meaning "Woodlands") is a vast, waterlogged region of eastern Europe, the largest swamp of the European continent. The Pripet Marshes occupy southern Belarus and northern Ukraine. They lie in the thickly forested basin of the Pripet River (a major tributary of the Dnieper) and are bounded on the north by the Belarusian Ridge and on the south by the Volyn-Podilsk and Dnieper uplands. The marshes cover an area of approximately 270,000 square km (104,000 square miles). The distinctive natural traits of the Pripet Marshes are a wide development of saturated sandy lowlands, intersected by a dense network of rivers with weakly cut riverbeds and wide floodlands; and a prevalence of pine forests amid the wide expanse of low-lying bogs and marshes.

The region experiences a warm temperate climate. The average annual precipitation reaches 550–650 mm

(22–26 inches) and exceeds evaporation, giving sufficient—and in some places quite abundant—moisture. Combined with an abundance of subsoil waters and their proximity to the surface, a virtually unique soil saturation and associated bogging down of the surface are thus produced.

Numerous tributaries of the Pripet (including the Stokhid, Styr, Horyn [Goryn], Ubort, Yaselda, and Ptich rivers) course down into the swamps from the surrounding highlands, carrying in large amounts of water. In the spring, when snowmelt occurs, the region's rivers overflow their low banks and intensify the saturation of the land. Huge marshes are developed along the course of the Pripet itself, while the middle of the river is marked by the soggy expanses of the Pinsk Marshes. The numerous lakes that dot the landscape are in various stages of choking up into additional bogs.

About one-third of the region is forested, consisting of pine, birch, alder, oak, aspen, white spruce, and hornbeam. The region has thus supported—where conditions permit—a diversified lumbering industry. Elk, lynx, wolf, fox, wild boar, roe, beaver, badger, and weasel are to be seen and are sometimes hunted. A host of birds, including black grouse, orioles, hazel grouse, woodpeckers, owls, blue tits, and ducks, inhabit the forests and marshlands. These, too, are hunted. Human intervention is most evident, however, in the sections of the region that are being developed and transformed into agricultural lands, where rye, barley, wheat, flax, hemp, potatoes, a variety of vegetables, and fodder grasses are cultivated.

Land reclamation projects were first initiated in 1872 by a state-sponsored "western expedition for the drainage of swamps" led by the Russian scholar I.I. Zhilinsky. A vast amount of land reclamation has taken place during the 20th century. A complex series of measures for achieving this formidable goal was under way during the late 20th century. They included the regulation of water drainage and the construction of reservoirs on the rivers, the regulation of river channels, afforestation of sandy uplands, and the clearing of undesirable vegetative cover.

SUNDARBANS

The Sundarbans, formerly Sunderbunds, is a vast tract of forest and saltwater swamp forming the lower part of the Padma River (Ganges [Ganga] River) delta, extending roughly 260 km (160 miles) along the Bay of Bengal from the Hugli River estuary in India to the western segment of the Meghna River estuary in Bangladesh. The tract reaches inland for about 80 km (50 miles) at its broadest point. A network of estuaries, tidal rivers, and creeks intersected by numerous channels, it encloses flat, marshy islands covered with dense forests.

The name Sundarbans is perhaps derived from the term meaning "forest of *sundari*," a reference to the large mangrove trees that are most plentiful in the area. The forest passes into a mangrove swamp along the coast, with many wild animals and crocodile-infested estuaries in its southern region. The area has long had the status of a forest reserve and also is one of the last preserves of the Bengal tiger (*Panthera tigris tigris*). In 1997 the mangrove forest of the Sundarbans was designated a UNESCO World Heritage site.

ZOIGÊ MARSH

The Zoigê Marsh—Chinese: (Pinyin) Ruo'ergai Zhaoze or (Wade-Giles romanization) Jo-erh-kai Chao-tse—which is also referred to as the Songpan Grasslands, is a large marsh lying mostly in northern Sichuan province in west-central China. It occupies about 2,600 square km (1,000 square miles) of the eastern part of the Plateau of Tibet at an elevation of 3,600 metres (11,800 feet) above sea level and extends westward across the border of Sichuan into southern Gansu and southeastern Qinghai provinces. The marsh, formed by abundant rain and snow, lies in a region of restricted drainage with a long frost period (fewer than 20 frost-free days annually). It is bordered on the east by the Min Mountains and on the west by the A'nyêmaqên (Amne Machin) Mountains; the Huang He (Yellow River) runs through the western part of the region from south to north. Beneath its uneven surface lies a layer of peat generally 2–3 metres (7–10 feet) thick but increasing to as much as 6–7 metres (20–23 feet) deep in some places. Crossed by the Chinese communists during the Long March (1934–35), the region was then a marshy wilderness area. In the 1970s ditches were dug, parts of the marsh were drained, and cattle, sheep, and horses pastured on the reclaimed grasslands. A nature preserve was established in the area in 1994. It is home to the chital, or spotted deer, and the black-necked crane.

CONCLUSION

Lakes and wetlands are significant reservoirs of life. In terms of primary productivity, lakes are comparable to temperate grasslands. Swamps and marshes, however, are five times more productive than lakes and are considered to be the most productive ecosystems on the planet. The tremendous amount of vegetable biomass produced in swamps and marshes supports a vibrant animal community made up of many terrestrial and aquatic species.

Like other ecosystems, many lake and wetland ecosystems have been altered by human activities. One of the most serious threats to lake and wetland ecosystems is caused by fertilizer runoff from agriculture and residential areas. Chemicals from these sources contain high amounts of phosphorous, nitrogen, or other compounds the plants require for growth. When these nutrients enter lakes and wetlands, aquatic plants and algae respond opportunistically and their growth accelerates. Later, population explosions of these photosynthetic organisms can choke the waterways where they occur.

This clogging of waterways is often seen as a minor nuisance, but exploding populations of aquatic plants may become a major ecological problem when these organisms shed tissues or die at the end of the growing season. As leaves, stems, and other tissues are cast off into the water, they sink and decompose. The process of breaking down so much plant material uses up much of the dissolved oxygen supply in the water. Many aquatic animals, such as fish and aquatic insects, that rely on dissolved oxygen, suddenly find themselves in low oxygen or anoxic (no oxygen) conditions that threaten their immediate survival.

Lakes and wetlands are also threatened by habitat loss associated with human activity. Throughout history, wetlands have been drained to increase farmland acreage. The rivers that irrigate wetlands and bring upstream water to lakes are often diverted to irrigate farmland, cool industrial machinery, reduce downstream flooding risk, or facilitate boat and barge transportation. Deprived of this critical resource, several lakes and wetlands have dried up, the most notable example of this phenomenon being the shrinkage of the Aral Sea in Central Asia.

Not all human activity has had a negative impact on these vital ecosystems. Individual countries, local grassroots organizations, and international groups such as the International Union for Conservation of Nature and Natural Resources have interceded on the behalf of many lakes and wetlands. Projects aimed at reducing pollution, diminishing the effect of invasive plant species, or creating wildlife sanctuaries are examples of humankind's desire to protect and preserve these important natural resources for many future generations to come.

APPENDIX A
NOTABLE SMALLER LAKES OF THE WORLD

HONGZE LAKE

Hongze Lake—Chinese: (Pinyin) Hongze Hu or (Wade-Giles romanization) Hung-tse Hu—is a large lake in the Huai River valley on the border between Jiangsu and Anhui provinces in eastern China. It was given the name Hongze Lake by the emperor Yangdi (reigned 604–617/618 CE) of the Sui dynasty (581–618).

In Tang and early Song times (from the 7th to the 10th century) it was smaller than its present surface area of 1,960 square km (757 square miles), probably less than a third of its present size. It was also separated from the main course of the Huai River, which flowed to the south and southeast of the lake. The Huai was shallow and difficult to navigate. In the 11th century, under the Song dynasty (960–1279), various canals were constructed to make use of the lake as a part of the canal system between Kaifeng (in Henan province) and Chuzhou (modern Huai'an; in Jiangsu province), joining the lake to the Huai. When, in 1194, the Huang He (Yellow River) changed its course to the south to join the Huai at modern Qingjiang (in Jiangsu), it usurped the lower course of the Huai, which no longer had a direct outlet to the sea. The waters of the Huai discharged into Hongze Lake, which then grew to its present size, inundating a vast area of fertile irrigated land. The surplus waters of the lake flowed southeast, via the Gaobao and Baoying lakes and the channel of the Grand Canal to the Yangtze River (Chang Jiang), east of Yangzhou (in Jiangsu).

Over the course of centuries, the lake's bottom silted up. By the 19th century, flooding in the area was frequent and severe. In the 1930s a new channel was dug from the eastern shore of the lake directly to the sea. This canal was restored and improved in 1951–52 under the name of the Subei Canal, and, together with the comprehensive water conservancy project for the Huai River valley, it has reduced flooding. The lake surface is only some 15 metres (50 feet) above sea level, however, and drainage remains a problem. Most of the lake is too shallow for any but small boats.

KOKO NOR

Koko Nor—Chinese: (Pinyin) Qinghai Hu or (Wade-Giles romanization) Ch'ing-hai Hu; Tibetan: Tso Ngömpo; English: Blue Lake—is a lake in Qinghai province of west-central China. The largest mountain lake without a river outlet in Central Asia, it is located in a depression of the Qilian Mountains, its surface at an elevation of about 3,200 metres (10,500 feet) above sea level.

The length of the lake approaches 105 km (65 miles) and the width 65 km (40 miles); the surface area of the lake is approximately 6,000 square km (about 2,300 square miles) in years when the water level is high and about 4,200 square km (1,600 square miles) when the level is low. The greatest known depth is about 38 metres (125 feet). However, measurements of the lake since the 1990s have indicated that the average water level has been dropping; at times, small areas of water have become isolated from the lake's main body in shallower coastline stretches. The water is azure in colour, and the name of the lake is derived from the Mongolian words meaning "blue lake."

The Koko Nor depression originated some 2.5 million years ago. The lake that formed in the depression originally drained into the Machu River, but uplift of the surrounding mountains cut off this outlet. Meltwaters from ancient glaciers thus accumulated and formed a larger, deeper lake in the late Pleistocene Epoch (i.e., at least 11,700 years ago). At that time the lake was nearly one-third wider than it is today and almost 50 metres (160 feet) deep. When the glaciers subsequently melted away, the lake dropped to its present level.

The land north of the depression containing the lake is rolling and hilly, with many low mountains. The depression is bordered on the south by the South Qinghai Mountains (South Koko Nor Mountains), which run as far as the eastern edge of the lake and form a narrow chain with distinct peaks that are continually snowcapped. Farther to the east the range drops off sharply into low hills. The rocks lining the depression consist mainly of red and gray sandstone and light-gray, claylike limestones. Traces of prehistoric human activity have been found in mountain loesses.

The Buha River empties into the western part of the lake, the resulting delta protruding southeastward toward the centre of the lake. Along the adjacent shores woods cover terraces that ascend from the shoreline to a height of 50 metres (160 feet) above the lake. On the eastern shore there are many small, isolated lakes and a rising, wooded shore. Numerous sandy islands dot the lake; the largest is 1,650 metres (5,410 feet) long and more than 300 metres (1,000 feet) wide. Bottom deposits consist mainly of black, yellow, and pale yellow silts; sand can be found in places, but close to the shore pebbles predominate. The mineral content of the water changes greatly from year to year, but salt (sodium chloride) is always present, and the water is brackish with a salinity of about 15 grams per litre (2 ounces per gallon) and is not potable. Of some two dozen rivers and streams that empty into the Koko Nor, the Buha River is the biggest. These rivers flow fastest in summer, raising the lake level. However, these streams (including the Buha) occasionally dry up for periods of time, the result of their water being diverted for irrigation and a general decline in precipitation in the region.

The Koko Nor basin has a comparatively dry climate. Snowstorms during the winter rage through the first half of March, although snow accumulation is not great. Most precipitation (more than 70 percent) occurs in July and August. On the southwest shore of the lake and on the slopes of the South Qinghai Mountains annual precipitation is 250 to 300 mm (10 to 12 inches); on the northern shore it is 350 to 400 mm (14 to 16 inches), and annual precipitation in the mountains to the north of the depression is up to 500 mm (20 inches). During the summer, water in the lake warms to 18–20 °C (64–68 °F). From November to March the lake surface freezes, the ice becoming as much as 60 cm (2 feet) thick.

Adjacent to the lake are luxuriant steppe grasses of various types, providing one of the best grazing areas around the South Qinghai Mountains. The principal forms of vegetation are wormwood (absinthe) and derris. Numerous other plants are present, including nettles, hollyhocks, and asters. Fir forests grow in the mountains.

Fish in the lake belong mainly to the carp family. Few large wild mammals inhabit the area because of the human presence in the territory, but the kiang (Asiatic wild ass) and the Przewalski's horse are found there. Blue sheep (oaran-kukuyaman) live in the mountains, as do wolves. The waterfront and the adjacent slopes are inhabited by a large variety of birds, including skylarks, grouse, sandpipers, cormorants, falcons, eagles, gray geese, and a few types of duck and gull. The scenic Bird Island is located at the northwest corner of the lake. The lake became a focus of attention in the early 21st century after an outbreak of avian influenza.

In addition to the Han (Chinese), various national minorities, including Tibetans, Mongols, and Hui (Chinese

Muslims), live along the shores. There are some settlements, including Jiangxigou and Heimahe, along the road from Xining to Lhasa, close to the southern shore of the lake. On the northern shore lies the settlement of Gangcha. Most of the non-Han peoples in the area, notably the Tibetans and Mongols, are nomads, who care for large numbers of cattle, sheep, horses, and camels.

LAKE COMO

Lake Como (Italian: Lago di Como, also called Lario; Latin: Lacus Larius) is a lake in Lombardy, northern Italy, 40 km (25 miles) north of Milan. It lies at an elevation of 199 metres (653 feet) in a depression surrounded by limestone and granite mountains that reach an elevation of about 600 metres (2,000 feet) in the south and more than 2,400 metres (8,000 feet) in the northeast. Lake Como has three branches of approximately equal length (about 26 km [16 miles]). One stretches northward past Colico; of the other two, one stretches southwestward to the city of Como, the other southeastward beyond Lecco (this branch also known as Lecco Lake), with Bellagio Promontory marking the bifurcation.

Lake Como is about 47 km (29 miles) long and up to 4 km (2.5 miles) wide, with an area of 146 square km (56 square miles) and a maximum depth of 414 metres (1,358 feet). It receives the Adda River, which enters it near Colico and issues from it at Lecco, and also the waters of numerous other rivers and mountain streams, including the Mera. It is subject to frequent floods and is swept by two winds, the *tivano* from the north in the morning and the *breva* from the south in the afternoon. Its northern arm once probably extended as far as Chiavenna, enclosing the area now covered by Mezzola Lake. Como is associated with the classical writings of Virgil, the two Plinys, and Claudian.

A luxuriant lakeshore vegetation includes vines and fig, pomegranate, olive, chestnut, and oleander trees. There is fishing for trout, eel, and *agoni,* a type of herring, but pollution has much reduced the fish population. The lake is famous for the natural beauty of its setting and for the handsome villas on its shores. Among the many noted lakeside resorts are Como, Lecco, Bellagio, Tremezzo, Menaggio, and Varenna. Several towns are connected by steamer services.

LAKE CONSTANCE

Lake Constance (German: Bodensee; Latin: Lacus Brigantinus), which is also called Lake of Constance, is a lake bordering Switzerland, Germany, and Austria and occupying an old glacier basin at an elevation of 396 metres (1,299 feet). It has an area of 541 square km (209 square miles) and is about 65 km (40 miles) long and up to 13 km (8 miles) wide, with an average depth of 90 metres (295 feet) and a maximum depth of 252 metres (827 feet). It has about 200 km (125 miles) of shoreline. In the west, near Konstanz (Constance), it is divided by the Bodan mountain ridge into two parts: the Unter Lake (south) and the Überlinger Lake (north). The lake's main body southeast of Konstanz is called the Ober Lake.

The lake forms part of the course of the Rhine River, which enters it in the southeast near Bregenz and leaves it at the west via the Unter Lake. The island of Mainau is north of Konstanz in the Überlinger Lake, and the island of Reichenau is west of the city in the Unter Lake. Konstanz itself is a "political island," for it is the only part of Germany on the lake's southwestern shore; it is entirely surrounded by Swiss territory, except on the northeast where it fronts on the lake.

The name Bodensee probably derives from the Carolingian imperial palatinate of Bodman at the northwest end of the Überlinger Lake. By the Middle Ages, the lake was a major traffic centre as the meeting place of roads from all directions. There are remains of Neolithic lake dwellings in the area.

The lake stores and reflects heat, contributing to the unusually sunny and mild climate along its shores. The fertile slopes along its shores support fruit-growing and wine production, and there is fishing for lake trout and salmon. Spectacular Alpine scenery combines with the mild climate to make the lake a popular resort area. The major lakeside cities are Konstanz, Lindau, and Friedrichshafen, Ger.; Bregenz, Austria; and Kreuzlingen, Switz.

LAKE EDWARD

Lake Edward (French: Lac Édouard) is one of the great lakes of the Western Rift Valley in eastern Africa. It lies astride the border of Congo (Kinshasa) and Uganda at an elevation of 912 metres (2,992 feet) and is 77 km (48 miles) long and 42 km (26 miles) wide. On the northeast it is connected to the smaller Lake George. The two lakes have a combined surface area of 2,500 square km (970 square miles). From Lake George, which receives the Ruwenzori River, water flows through the 32-km (20-mile)-long Kazinga Channel to Lake Edward, also fed by the Rutshuru River (crossing a wide plain in the south). Lake Edward empties northward through the Semliki River to Lake Albert (after 1973, also called Lake Mobutu Sese Seko), the waters of which empty as the Albert Nile. Lake Edward's northern and southern shores are low plains, but most of its east and west banks are steep trough walls. To the north, the Ruwenzori Range rises to 5,119 metres (16,795 feet) at Margherita Peak. The lake abounds in fish; wildlife about its shores is protected within Congo's Virunga National Park and Uganda's Queen Elizabeth (Ruwenzori) National Park.

Lake George was visited in 1875 by Henry (later Sir Henry) Morton Stanley, who named it Beatrice Gulf (for a daughter of Queen Victoria) in the belief that it was part of Lake Albert. In 1888–89 Stanley ascended the Semliki to Lake Edward, which he named after Albert Edward, Prince of Wales (later Edward VII).

LAKE EYRE

Lake Eyre is a great salt lake in central South Australia, with a total area of 9,300 square km (3,700 square miles). It lies in the southwestern corner of the Great Artesian Basin, a closed inland basin about 1,140,000 square km (440,150 square miles) in area that is drained only by intermittent streams. Normally dry but susceptible to occasional flooding, the lake constitutes the lowest point on the Australian continent. Lake Eyre was first sighted by a European in 1840—Edward John Eyre, after whom it was named. The lake's extent had been determined by the 1870s.

Lake Eyre, the lowest part of which lies about 15 metres (50 feet) below sea level, consists of two sections. Lake Eyre North, 144 km (90 miles) long and 65 km (40 miles) wide, is joined by the narrow Goyder Channel to Lake Eyre South, which is 65 km long and about 24 km (15 miles) in width.

Evidence from the western side of Lake Eyre strongly suggests that the present saline depression resulted from a downfaulting in the Earth's surface about 30,000 years ago, which blocked off an earlier outlet to the sea. Water reaching the lake now evaporates very rapidly, and the surface of the lake bed has a thin crust of salt deposited by water that has evaporated.

Lake Eyre is normally dry; it fills completely only an average of twice in a century, but partial, minor fillings happen much more often. When completely filled (as in 1950, 1974, and 1984), the lake takes about two years to dry up again. Lake Eyre is in a region of very low and intermittent rainfall amounting to less than 125 mm (5 inches) annually. The lake is fed by a vast internal continental drainage basin, but evaporation rates in the region are so high that most of the rivers in the basin dry up before reaching the lake. Thus, the waters of the Diamantina and other rivers can feed the lake only when they are in flood after heavy rains.

The thin salt crust of Lake Eyre thickens in the lake's southern portions, where it is as much as 46 cm (18 inches) thick. The extremely level surface of the salt crust has been used in attempts to break world land-speed records, notably in 1964, when Donald Campbell drove at a speed of more than 644 km (400 miles) per hour in *Bluebird II*.

LAKE GARDA

Lake Garda (Italian: Lago Di Garda, also called Benaco) is the largest (area 370 square km [143 square miles]) of the Italian lakes. It borders Lombardy (southwest and west), Veneto (east and southeast), and Trentino-Alto Adige (north). It is surpassed in area in the Alpine region only by Lakes Geneva and Constance. Lying at an elevation of 65 metres (213 feet), the lake is 54 km (34 miles) long and 3–18 km (2–11 miles) wide, with a shoreline of 125 km (77.5 miles) and a maximum depth of 346 metres (1,135 feet). Separated from the Adige River valley by the narrow ridge of Mount Baldo, the lake is fed by the Sarca River at its northern end, while the Mincio flows out toward the Po River at the southern end. Narrow at the northern end, between towering cliffs, the lake widens gradually southward into a nearly circular basin, with rich vegetation on the southern and western shores. The predominant winds (which may swell into violent storms) are the *sover* from the north in the morning and the *ora* from the south in the afternoon.

The lake was called Lacus Benacus by the classical writers Virgil, Horace, and Catullus; its name was changed when the city of Garda, elevated to a county in the early 9th century by the emperor Charlemagne, acquired dominion over the lake. The northern end belonged to Austria until 1919. The lake is encircled by the magnificent Gardesana scenic route (143 km [89 miles]), opened in 1931. Well sheltered by the Alps to the north, Lake Garda has a temperate Mediterranean climate, which makes it a popular resort area. Citrus fruits, olives, vines, laurels, oleanders, cypresses, and palms are grown on the southern and western shores, and there is fishing for eels, carp, and trout. Small steamers ply between the principal lakeside towns of Riva, Gargnano, Desenzano del Garda, and Peschiera del Garda.

LAKE GENEVA

Lake Geneva (French: Lac Léman, or Lac de Genève; German: Genfersee) is the largest Alpine lake in Europe (area 581 square km [224 square miles]), lying between southwestern Switzerland and Haute-Savoie *département*, southeastern France. About 347 square km (134 square miles) of the lake's area are Swiss, and 234 square km (90 square miles) are French. Crescent in shape, the lake is formed by the Rhône River, which enters it at the east end between Villeneuve, Switz., and Saint-Gingolph, France, and leaves it at the west end through the city of Geneva.

The only important tributaries are the Dranse (south) and the Venoge (north).

Lying at an elevation of 372 metres (1,220 feet), the lake is 72 km (45 miles) long, with a maximum width of 13.5 km (8.5 miles) and an average width of 8 km (5 miles). The maximum depth is 310 metres (1,017 feet), the mean depth 80 metres (262 feet). The strait of Promenthoux, or Nernier, separates the lake into two well-marked divisions, the Grand Lac (east) and the Petit Lac, the special Genevese portion. The water, unusually blue and transparent, is subject to remarkable fluctuations of level known as seiches, in which the whole fluid mass in the lake rhythmically swings from shore to shore. The lake is not as rich in fish as the other Swiss lakes. There are known to be 20 indigenous species, and six that were introduced in the 19th century.

Prehistoric lake dwellings have been found on the shores. The Lacus Lemanus of classical Latin writers, it was known from the 16th century as the Lac de Genève, but the name Lac Léman was revived from the end of the 18th century.

The north shore forms a fertile wine-producing hinterland rising to the Jura Mountains, whereas the south and east shores are bordered by the Savoy and Valaisan Alps. Geneva and Lausanne are the largest lakeside cities, and there are numerous resorts, including Montreux and Vevey in Switzerland and Thonon-les-Bains and Évian-les-Bains in France.

LAKE LADOGA

Lake Ladoga (Russian: Ladozhskoye Ozero or Ladozhskoe Ozero) is the largest lake in Europe, located in northwestern Russia about 40 km (25 miles) east of St. Petersburg. It is 17,600 square km (6,700 square miles) in area—exclusive of islands—and 219 km (136 miles) long, with an average width of 82 km (51 miles) and an average depth of 51 metres (167 feet). Its greatest depth, at a point west of Valaam Island, is 230 metres (754 feet).

Lake Ladoga's basin has a total area of about 259,000 square km (100,000 square miles). The depression of the lake was produced by the action of glaciers. The northern shores are mostly high and craggy and are broken by deep, ice-covered, fjordlike inlets. There are numerous, mostly wooded islands there, with cliffs. The southern shores, which have many sandy or rocky beaches, are primarily low, slightly indented, and overgrown with willows and alders. In some places there are ancient coastal embankments overgrown with pines. There are approximately 50,000 lakes and 3,500 rivers more than 10 km (6 miles) long in the Lake Ladoga basin. The largest tributaries are the Volkhov, the Svir, and the Vuoksa.

The lake also contains approximately 660 islands of more than 1 hectare (2.5 acres) in area, occupying a total of 456 square km (176 square miles). The largest islands are Riyekkalan-Sari, Mantsinsari, Kilpola, Tulolansari, and Valaam.

The climate in the Lake Ladoga region is moderately cold. Mean annual precipitation is 610 mm (24 inches). The lake is highest in June and July and lowest in December and January; its average annual range of elevation is about 0.8 metres (2.6 feet), and the absolute maximum annual variation was about 3 metres (9.8 feet). Seiches, or temporary, sometimes drastic changes in the water level, can be observed.

Thermal conditions differ from the deep central to the shallow coastal regions of the lake. The coastal regions and inlets usually freeze at the beginning of December, and the open central area freezes in January or February; the average ice thickness is 50–60 cm (20–23 inches). The central part of the lake opens in late March or early April, the northern part not until the beginning of May.

Lake Ladoga's water, yellow-brown in colour, is fresh, with an average mineralization of about 56 parts per million of calcium hydrocarbonate. The lake abounds in fish of commercial importance. Water transportation and fishing are the principal commercial uses of Lake Ladoga. The lake is part of the Volga–Baltic water route and of the White Sea–Baltic Waterway system, through which freight is carried, without the need for transshipment, to points within Russia and to Finland, Germany, and other countries.

During World War II, when Leningrad (St. Petersburg) was under siege by the Germans from September 1941 to March 1943, Lake Ladoga was the lifeline connecting it with the rest of the Soviet Union. Supplies and military equipment were brought to the city across the water and ice, and the sick and wounded were evacuated over the same route.

The cities of Priozyorsk, Shlisselburg, and Sortavala are located on its shores.

LAKE MAGGIORE

Lake Maggiore (Italian: Lago Maggiore; Latin: Lacus Verbanus) is the second largest lake in Italy (area 212 square km [82 square miles]); it is bisected by the border between Lombardy (east) and Piedmont (west). Its northern end is in the Swiss Ticino *canton*. At an elevation of 193 metres (633 feet) above sea level, the lake is 54 km (34 miles) long, with a maximum width of 11 km (7 miles) and a maximum depth of 372 metres (1,220 feet). The lake is traversed from north to south by the Ticino River, and its other principal affluents are the Maggia from the north, the Toce from the west, and the short Tresa from Lake

Lugano on the east. Off the western shore are the famous Borromean Islands, geologic continuations of the Pallanza Promontory. Lake Maggiore is bordered by the Swiss Alps to the north and by the Lombardian Plain and has a warm, mild climate.

The greatest landowners around the lake since the 15th century have been the Borromeo family, who still own the islands and fishery rights. The lake's name, meaning "greater," refers to its being considerably larger than the neighbouring Orta and Varese lakes.

There is fishing for trout, pike, perch, and shad. Well-known lakeside resorts on the western shore are Stresa, Verbania, Arona, and Cannobio. Other towns are Luino and Laveno, on the eastern shore, and Locarno, Switz., at the northern end. Small steamers ply between them. Southwest of Verbania, Mount Mottarone (1,491 metres [4,892 feet]) rises between Lake Maggiore and Lake Orta.

LAKE MARACAIBO

Lake Maracaibo (Spanish: Lago de Maracaibolarge) is an inlet of the Caribbean Sea, lying in the Maracaibo Basin of northwestern Venezuela. It is the largest natural lake in South America, covering an area of about 13,300 square km (5,150 square miles), extending southward for 210 km (130 miles) from the Gulf of Venezuela, and reaching a width of 121 km (75 miles). Many rivers flow into Lake Maracaibo, the most important being the Catatumbo River, a transportation artery for products from the adjacent regions and from the Colombian-Venezuelan highlands. The lake water in the southern portion is fresh, but a stronger tidal influence makes the northern waters somewhat brackish. The lake is quite shallow, except toward the south, and it is surrounded by swampy lowlands. For many years a bar at the mouth of the lake, extending some 26 km (16 miles), restricted navigation to vessels drawing less than 4 metres (13 feet) of water. After constant dredging in the 1930s had increased the depth to 8 metres (25 feet), a 3-km (2-mile)-long stone breakwater and a 11-metre- (35-foot-) deep channel were completed in 1957 to accommodate oceangoing ships and tankers.

Lake Maracaibo is one of the world's richest and most centrally located petroleum-producing regions. The first productive well was drilled in 1917, and the productive area has come to include a 105-km (65-mile) strip along the eastern shore, extending 32 km (20 miles) out into the lake. Thousands of derricks protrude from the water, and many more line the shore, while underwater pipelines transport the petroleum to storage tanks on the land. The lake's basin supplies about two-thirds of the total Venezuelan petroleum output. Most of the industry was developed by foreign (chiefly American, British, and Dutch) investment, with very few locally owned wells, but in 1975 the petroleum industry was nationalized. Natural gas is also obtained.

LAKE MANAGUA

Lake Managua (Spanish: Lago De Managua) is a large lake in western Nicaragua. It rests in a rift valley at an elevation of 39 metres (128 feet) above sea level. The lake, 20 metres (65 feet) in depth, is 58 km (36 miles) from east to west and 25 km (16 miles) from north to south; its area is 1,035 square km (400 square miles). Also known by its Indian name, Xolotlán, the lake is fed by numerous streams rising in the central highlands and the Diriamba Highlands. It is drained by the Tipitapa River, which flows into Lake Nicaragua.

The lake is economically significant: its waters yield fish and alligators and are plied by shallow-draft vessels. Momotombo Volcano, reaching 1,280 metres (4,199 feet) above sea level, is on the northwestern shore. Managua, the national capital, lies along the lake's southern shore. In 1998 the rains caused by Hurricane Mitch (approximately 1,900 mm [75 inches] over five days), one of the Atlantic Ocean's deadliest tropical cyclones, overflowed Lake Managua and inundated several of the poorest communities in the area.

LAKE NASSER

Lake Nasser, which is also called Lake Nubia, is a reservoir on the Nile River in Upper Egypt and northern Sudan. It was created by the impounding of the Nile's waters by the Aswan High Dam, which was built in the 1960s and dedicated in 1971. Lake Nasser has a gross capacity of 168,900,000,000 cubic metres (136,927,000 acre-feet), and its waters, when discharged downstream, have brought 324,000 hectares (800,000 acres) of additional land under irrigation and have converted 283,000 hectares (700,000 acres) from flood to perennial irrigation. The lake has been stocked with food fish.

The creation of the lake threatened to submerge a number of significant historical sites—notably the tombs and temples at Philae and Abu Simbel—under its waters. The Egyptian government appealed to UNESCO, with whose assistance many monuments were dismantled and reconstructed on safer ground. In the early 1980s land-reclamation projects began in the desert around the lake. The northern two-thirds of the lake, lying in Egypt, is named for Gamal Abdel Nasser, president (1956–70); the southern third, in the Sudan, is called Lake Nubia.

LAKE NICARAGUA

Lake Nicaragua (Spanish: Lago de Nicaragua) is the largest of several freshwater lakes in southwestern Nicaragua and the dominant physical feature of the country. It is also the largest lake in Central America. Its indigenous name is Cocibolca, and the Spanish called it Mar Dulce—both terms meaning "sweet sea." Its present name is said to have been derived from that of Nicarao, an Indian chief whose people lived on the lake's shores.

Oval in shape, with an area of 8,157 square km (3,149 square miles), the lake is 177 km (110 miles) in length and has an average width of 58 km (36 miles). It is about 18 metres (60 feet) deep in the centre, and its waters reach a depth of 60 metres (200 feet) to the southeast of its largest island, Ometepe. The lake's surface is 29 metres (95 feet) above sea level.

It is believed that Lake Nicaragua, together with Lake Managua to the northwest, originally formed part of an ocean bay that, as a result of volcanic eruption, became an inland basin containing the two lakes, which are linked by the Tipitapa River. The ocean fish thus trapped adapted themselves as the salt water gradually turned fresh. Lake Nicaragua is the only freshwater lake containing oceanic animal life, including sharks, swordfish, and tarpon.

More than 40 rivers drain into the lake, the largest being the Tipitapa River. The San Juan River drains out of the lake, following a 180-km (112-mile) course that runs from the southeastern shore of the lake through a densely forested region to empty into the Caribbean Sea. For part of its course, the San Juan forms the boundary between Nicaragua and Costa Rica. To the southwest, the lake is separated from the Pacific Ocean by a narrow land corridor, the Rivas Isthmus, which is 19 km (12 miles) wide.

Contrary to popular belief, the lake is tideless, although there is a daily fluctuation in the water level caused by east winds blowing up the San Juan valley. The water level also falls during the dry season, December to April, and rises during the rainy season, May to October. There are several currents in the lake; the principal one runs from southeast to northeast on the surface, while beneath it a deeper current flows in the opposite direction. Surface water temperature usually remains near 24 °C (75 °F), and bottom temperature stays near 16 °C (60 °F). Due to the chemical composition of the volcanic rocks forming parts of the lake's bed and shores, the lake waters contain high proportions of dissolved magnesium and potassium salts.

There are more than 400 islands in the lake, 300 of which are within 8 km (5 miles) of the city of Granada on the northwest shore. Most of the islands are covered with a rich growth of vegetation, which includes tropical fruit trees. Some of the islands are inhabited. Ometepe is 26 km (16 miles) long and 13 km (8 miles) wide. It is formed of what originally were two separate volcanoes — Concepción, which is 1,610 metres (5,282 feet) high and last erupted in 1983, and Madera, which is 1,394 metres (4,573 feet) high. Lava from bygone eruptions forms a bridge between them, called the Tistian Isthmus. A third volcano associated with the lake is Mombacho, about 1,350 metres (4,430 feet) high, which stands on the western shore. Ometepe Island is the preeminent site in Nicaragua for pre-Columbian examples of statuary, ceramics, and other archaeological remains, some of which are believed to represent vestiges of ancient South American, as well as North American, civilizations.

In previous centuries, piratical raids from the Caribbean were sometimes made on the lakeside towns, until the building of fortifications in the 17th century on the San Juan River blocked the pirates' ingress. From the time of the ending of Spanish rule in the 1820s, the possibility of constructing a canal across Nicaragua from the Atlantic to the Pacific — a route that would run up the San Juan River, cross the lake, and be completed by a channel dug through the Rivas Isthmus — has been mooted. After the discovery of gold in California in 1848, Cornelius Vanderbilt, the New York millionaire, developed the Vanderbilt Road—a route over which gold prospectors from New York were transported up the river and over the lake, completing the final few miles to the Pacific by stagecoach in order to take ship to San Francisco. The arrangement revived interest—which lasted for many years—in the possibilities of a trans-Nicaragua canal. After the completion of the Panama Canal in 1914, interest in the project once more subsided. Nevertheless, by the provisions of the Bryan-Chamorro Treaty (1914), concluded between Nicaragua and the United States, the United States had the exclusive right to build such a canal until 1970, when the treaty was abrogated.

LAKE ONEGA

Lake Onega (Russian: Onezhskoye or Ozero Onezhskoe) is the second largest lake in Europe. It is situated in the northwest part of the European portion of Russia between Lake Ladoga and the White Sea. It covers an area of 9,720 square km (3,753 square miles). It is 248 km (154 miles) long; its greatest width is 80 km (50 miles); and its greatest depth is about 116 metres (380 feet).

The hollow of the lake was formed by movements of the Earth's crust, but Quaternary glaciers (those from the past 2.6 million years) elongated it from northwest to southeast. The shores to the north and northwest are high and rocky, built of layered granite and covered with forest. There are deep bays at Petrozavodsk, Kondopoga, and Povenots. The southern shores are narrow, sandy, and often marshy or flooded. Onega has about 1,650 islands covering a total of approximately 260 square km (100 square miles), mostly in the northern and northwestern bays.

Fifty rivers enter Onega, the largest being the Shuya and Suna in the northwest and the Vodla in the east. In the southeast and east are the Andoma, Vytegra, and Megra rivers. Lake Onega itself empties into the Svir River. The water level reaches its highest point in the summer and its lowest in March–April, varying about 60 cm (24 inches) annually. The water circulates in a twisting pattern within the lake because of differences of temperature between the coastal and the open regions. During autumn gales, waves sometimes reach about 4.5 metres (some 14 or 15 feet).

The region has a cold climate. The coastal parts of the lake and the small bays begin to freeze at the end of November, and the deeper central parts in the middle of January, although in some years the central parts do not freeze. Thawing begins at the end of April.

The colour of Onega's water is dark yellowish brown in the open part and grayish brown along the shores. The lake contains more than 40 species of fish, including ryapushka (a small member of the salmon family), smelt, burbot (a freshwater variant of the cod), bream, pike, perch, roach, and salmon. The fish are of considerable economic value.

Lake Onega is connected with the Baltic and White seas by the White Sea–Baltic Canal and with the basin of the Volga River by the Volga-Baltic Waterway, which enable it to play an important part in both internal and international transportation. Goods are shipped over this route from Finland, Sweden, Denmark, and Germany to points in the east and north. For protection against storms, a bypass canal has been dug along the south and southeastern shores from the mouth of the Vytegra River to the source of the Svir. The cities of Petrozavodsk, Kondopoga, and Medvezhyegorsk are on Lake Onega. The island of Kizhi houses the internationally known architectural organization of that name.

LAKE RUDOLF

Lake Rudolf, which is also called Lake Turkana, is the fourth largest of the eastern African lakes. It lies mainly in northern Kenya, with its northern end stretching into Ethiopia. The lake lies in the eastern arm of eastern Africa's Rift Valley. It covers an area of 6,405 square km (2,473 square miles) and lies at 375 metres (1,230 feet) above sea level. Together with Lake Baringo (south), Lake Rudolf once formed a larger body of water drained by the Sobat River into the Nile River. Earth movements during the Pleistocene Epoch (about 2,600,000 to 11,700 years ago), however, created a smaller lake of independent inland drainage. Volcanic outcrops give rise to rocky shores in the east and south, while the lake's western and northern shores are lower and consist of sand dunes, sandspits, and mudflats. The three main islands in the lake—North, Central, and South—are volcanic.

Lake Rudolf is 248 km (154 miles) long, only 16–32 km (10–20 miles) wide, and relatively shallow, its greatest recorded depth being 73 metres (240 feet). The lake's level and area tend to fluctuate. Its only perennial tributary is the Omo River, which flows from Ethiopia. Having no outlet, the lake's waters are brackish. Sudden storms are frequent, rendering navigation on the lake treacherous.

Lake Rudolf is a rich reservoir of fish. Nile perch, tigerfish, bichir, and various species of *Tilapia* abound. Crocodiles and hippopotamuses are common, and birds include flamingos, cormorants, and kingfishers. The peoples of the neighbouring desert scrub are largely nomadic pastoralists. Count Samuel Teleki and Lieutenant Ludwig von Höhnel visited the lake in 1888 and named it after the crown prince of Austria. In Kenya it is called Lake Turkana.

LAKE TAI

Lake Tai—Chinese: (Pinyin) Tai Hu or (Wade-Giles romanization) T'ai Hularge—is a lake between Zhejiang and Jiangsu provinces in eastern China. Roughly crescent-shaped, it is about 70 km (45 miles) from north to south and 59 km (37 miles) from east to west; its total surface area is about 2,425 square km (935 square miles). The lake lies in a flat plain and is connected with a maze of water-ways that feed it from the west and discharge its waters eastward into the East China Sea, via the Wusong, Liu, Huangpu, and other rivers. In addition to these natural waterways, there is an intricate pattern of canals and irri-gation channels associated with the lake. Only on the northeast side is the lake bounded by uplands—a ridge of hills that also outcrop in the lake as islands, many of which, because of silting, have been joined to the shoreline.

The surrounding area has been settled since the 1st century BCE, but the irrigation system mostly dates from the 7th century CE and later. Reclamation and drainage improvements were conducted intensively between the 10th and 13th centuries; large-scale flood control measures were undertaken in the 11th and again in the 15th century. Similar improvements have been carried out in more recent times: drainage canals and dikes have been built, and an ever more complex irrigation pattern has emerged. In the 1930s the Chinese Nationalist government estab-lished a water conservancy authority for the lake that the Chinese communist government replaced after 1949 with a water conservancy assembly that also became respon-sible for the surrounding area.

Some of the islands in the eastern part of the lake are traditionally famous Daoist and Buddhist religious sites, and several thousand people live on them, raising fruit and fishing in the lake. Lake Tai has historically been considered a place of great natural beauty, and the area, particularly in the east near Suzhou and in the north around Wuxi (both in Jiangsu), attracts many tourists.

By the early 21st century, however, the improper disposal of chemicals and sewage had caused a toxic algae to form on the lake's surface, thereby threatening the quality of drinking water for people living nearby. In 2007 the Chinese government addressed growing concerns about Lake Tai's contamination when it pledged to spend more than $14 billion as part of a large-scale cleanup project. Many local factories were closed and water treatment regulations made more strict as part of a five-year plan to improve water quality.

LAKE TITICACA

Lake Titicaca (Spanish: Lago Titicaca) is the world's highest lake navigable to large vessels. The lake rests at 12,500 feet (3,810 metres) above sea level in the Andes Mountains of South America, astride the border between Peru to the west and Bolivia to the east. Titicaca is the second largest lake of South America (after Maracaibo). It covers some 8,300 square km (3,200 square miles) and extends in a northwest-to-southeast direction for a distance of 190 km (120 miles). It is 80 km (50 miles) across at its widest point. A narrow strait, Tiquina, separates the lake into two bodies of water. The smaller, in the southeast, is called Lake Huiñaymarca in Bolivia and Lake Pequeño in Peru; the larger, in the northwest, is called Lake Chucuito in Bolivia and Lake Grande in Peru.

The meaning of the name Titicaca is uncertain, but it has been variously translated as Rock of the Puma or Crag of Lead. Titicaca lies between Andean ranges in a vast basin (about 58,000 square km [22,400 square miles] in area) that comprises most of the Altiplano (High Plateau) of the central Andes. In the snow-covered Cordillera Real on the northeastern (Bolivian) shore of the lake, some of the highest peaks in the Andes rise to heights of more than 6,400 metres (21,000 feet).

The lake averages between 140 and 180 metres (460 and 600 feet) in depth, but the bottom tilts sharply toward the Bolivian shore, reaching its greatest recorded depth of 280 metres (920 feet) off Isla Soto in the lake's northeast corner.

More than 25 rivers empty their waters into Titicaca. The largest, the Ramis, draining about two-fifths of the entire Titicaca Basin, enters the northwestern corner of the lake. One small river, the Desaguadero, drains the lake at its southern end. This single outlet empties only 5 percent of the lake's excess water. The rest is lost by evaporation under the fierce sun and strong winds of the dry Altiplano.

Titicaca's level fluctuates seasonally and over a cycle of years. During the rainy season (summer, from December to March) the level of the lake rises, normally to recede during the dry winter months. It was formerly believed that Titicaca was slowly drying up, but modern studies have seemed to refute this, indicating a more or less regular cycle of rise and fall.

Titicaca's waters are limpid and only slightly brackish, with salinity ranging from 5.2 to 5.5 parts per 1,000. Surface temperatures average 14 °C (56 °F); from a thermocline at 20 metres (66 feet) temperatures drop to 11 °C (52 °F) at the bottom. Analyses show measurable quantities of sodium chloride, sodium sulfate, calcium sulfate, and magnesium sulfate in the water.

Lake Titicaca's fish life consists principally of two species of killifish (*Orestias*)—a small fish, usually striped or barred with black—and a catfish (*Trichomycterus*). In 1939, and subsequently, trout were introduced into Titicaca. A large frog (*Telmatobius*), which may reach a length of nearly a foot, inhabits the shallower regions of the lake.

Forty-one islands, some of them densely populated, rise from Titicaca's waters. The largest, Titicaca Island (Spanish: Isla de Titicaca, also called Isla del Sol), lies just off the tip of the Copacabana Peninsula in Bolivia.

Ruins on the shore and on the islands attest to the previous existence of one of the oldest civilizations known in the Americas. The chief site is at Tiwanaku, Bolivia, at the southern end of the lake. On Titicaca Island ruins of a temple mark the spot where, according to the tradition of the Incas (a Quechuan people of Peru who established an empire about 1100 CE), the legendary founders of the Inca dynasty, Manco Capac and Mama Ocllo, were sent down to Earth by the Sun.

The Aymara people living in the Titicaca Basin still practice their ancient methods of agriculture on stepped terraces that predate Inca times. They grow barley, quinoa (a type of pigweed that produces a small grain), and the potato, which originated on the Altiplano. The highest cultivated plot in the world was found near Titicaca—a field of barley growing at a height of 4,700 metres (15,420 feet) above sea level. At this elevation the grain never ripens, but the stalks furnish forage for llamas and alpacas, the American relatives of the camel that serve the Indians as beasts of burden and provide meat and wool. The lake plain is covered with vast numbers of pre-Columbian raised platform fields and ditches, now abandoned, which were constructed to improve drainage and enhance the region's agricultural potential. This ancient system of reclamation has been revived in some areas in both Peru and Bolivia.

The remnants of an ancient people, the Uru, still live on floating mats of dried totora (a reedlike papyrus that grows in dense brakes in the marshy shallows). From the totora, the Uru and other lake dwellers make their famed balsas—boats fashioned of bundles of dried reeds lashed together that resemble the crescent-shaped papyrus craft pictured on ancient Egyptian monuments.

In 1862 the first steamer to ply the lake was prefabricated in England and carried in pieces on muleback up to the lake. Today vessels make regular crossings from Puno, on the Peruvian shore, to the small Bolivian port of Guaqui. A narrow-gauge railway connects Guaqui with La Paz, capital of Bolivia. One of the world's highest railways runs from Puno down to Arequipa and the Pacific, completing for land-bound Bolivia, an important link with the sea, and also to Cuzco.

LAKE URMIA

Lake Urmia (Persian: Daryācheh-ye Orūmīyeh) sits in northwestern Iran. It is the largest lake in the Middle East and covers an area that varies from 5,200 to 6,000 square km (2,000 to 2,300 square miles). Like the Dead Sea, it is remarkable for the extreme salinity of its waters. Since 1967 it has enjoyed the status of a wetland protected region, and efforts have been made by the Iranian government to increase its wildlife.

The lake lies in the bottom of the large central depression of the Azerbaijan region in northwestern Iran, at an elevation of 1,275 metres (4,183 feet) above sea level. The basin is surrounded by mountains in the west and north, by plateaus in the south, and by plateaus and volcanic cones in the east. The lake is about 140 km (87 miles) long and 40 to 55 km (25 to 35 miles) wide, with a maximum depth of 16 metres (53 feet). In its southern portion there is a cluster of about 50 tiny islands. The shoreline varies with the lake level; when the water is high, it extends into large salt marshes to the east and south. The lake's shores are largely uninhabited.

The governing factor of Lake Urmia's hydrography is its lack of an outlet. It forms the dead end of a large drainage system that covers an area of about 52,000 square km (20,000 square miles) and is subject to great seasonal variation. The main affluents are the Talkheh (Ājī) River in the northeast, which gathers the melted snows from the Sabalān and Sahand massifs, and the twin rivers Zarīneh (Jagātu) and Sīmīneh (Tatavi) in the south.

The volume of water discharged into the lake by these rivers varies considerably during the year: during the spring the Talkheh River and Sīmīneh River may each discharge about 57 cubic metres (2,000 cubic feet) per second, while the rate drops to only 3.7 or 1.7 cubic metres (130 or 60 cubic feet) per second in the dry summer. This variation causes the lake itself to rise and fall, fluctuating by 0.6 to 0.9 metre (2 to 3 feet). In addition to seasonal variations, there are also longer periods of fluctuations, lasting from 12 to 20 years, with water-level fluctuations of 1.8 to 2.7 metres (6 to 9 feet).

Because Lake Urmia's waters have no outlet, they are highly saline. The lake is one-fourth as salty as the Dead Sea, with a salt content ranging from 8 to 11 percent in the spring to 26 or 28 percent in the late autumn. The main salts are chlorine, sodium, and sulfates.

Organic life in the lake's waters is limited to a few salt-tolerant species. Copious algae provide food for brine shrimp and cause a bad smell along the lake's shores. There are breeding populations of sheldrake, flamingo, and pelican, as well as migratory birds.

LAKE VAN

Lake Van (Turkish: Van Gölü) is the largest body of water in Turkey and the second largest in the Middle East. The lake is located in the region of eastern Anatolia near the border of Iran. It covers an area of 3,713 square km (1,434 square miles) and is more than 119 km (74 miles) across at its widest point. Known to the ancient Greek geographers as Thospitis Lacus, or Arsissa Lacus, its modern Turkish name, Van Gölü, is derived from Van, or Chauon, the name of the capital of the Urartian kingdom that flourished on the lake's eastern shore between the 10th and 8th centuries BCE. Roughly triangular in shape, the lake lies in an enclosed basin; its brackish waters are unsuitable for either drinking or irrigation. The salt water allows for no animal life save the *darekh* (related to the European bleak, a small soft-finned river fish of the carp family), a freshwater fish that has adapted to a saline environment.

Lake Van occupies the lowest part of a vast basin bordered by high mountains to the south, by plateaus and mountains to the east, and by a complex of volcanic cones to the west. At some time during the Pleistocene Epoch (i.e., about 2,600,000 to 11,700 years ago), a lava flow from the Nemrut volcano extended for nearly 60 km (37 miles) across the southwestern end of the basin, blocking westward drainage to the Murat River and thereby transforming the depression into a lake basin without outlet.

Lake Van is divided into two sections; the main body of water is separated from its much shallower northern extension by a narrow passage. Its shores are generally steep and lined with cliffs; the southern shore is extremely sinuous and eroded. The waters are dotted with islands, including Gadir, the largest, in the north; Çarpanak in the east; and Aktamar and Atrek in the south. The main body of the lake to the south is much deeper than its northern section, with the greatest depths exceeding 100 metres (330 feet).

Lake Van's catchment area exceeds 15,000 square km (5,790 square miles); it forms the largest interior basin of Turkey except for that of the central Anatolian region. The lake is fed by rainfall and meltwater as well as by several tributaries, notably the Bendimahi and Zilan rivers, which flow in from the north, and the Karasu and Micinger rivers, which enter the lake from the east. Lake Van experiences a seasonal variation of its water level of about 50 cm (20 inches) per year. It is lowest during the winter months and begins to rise after the spring thaw. With the arrival of additional water from the melted snows of the surrounding mountains, the lake rises to its highest level in July.

The lake has three distinct temperature zones in summer, consisting of an upper layer of warm water, a lower region of cold water, and an intermediate transitional layer. During the winter the surface cools quickly; occasionally the shallow northern sector freezes over. Freezing of the entire lake is retarded by its high salinity. The most abundant salts in the lake are sodium carbonate and sodium sulfate.

A regular passenger boat service plies the lake between the coastal towns; there is a small shipyard at Tuğ on the southwestern shore.

LAKE WINNIPEGOSIS

Lake Winnipegosis is a lake in western Manitoba, Can., situated between Lake Winnipeg and the Saskatchewan border. It is a remnant of glacial Lake Agassiz. Supplied by numerous small streams on the west, the 5,374-square-km (2,075-square-mile) lake is drained southeastward into Lake Manitoba and thence into Lake Winnipeg. Lake Winnipegosis is more than 240 km (150 miles) long, is up to 51 km (32 miles) wide, and has a maximum depth of 254 metres (833 feet). Winnipegosis (a Cree Indian term meaning "little muddy water") is an island-strewn lake that is navigable only by small vessels. It was explored in 1739 by the French fur trader La Vérendrye and later served as part of the major east-west canoe route of the North West Company. The lake is now important for commercial fishing, centred on the town of Winnipegosis. Although the population of wall-eye, sauger, pike, and perch has been on the decline, substantial efforts have been underway to bring specific populations back to normal numbers.

LAKE YSYK

Lake Ysyk (Kyrgyz: Ysyk-köl; Russian: Ozero Issyk-kul) is a drainless lake in northeastern Kyrgyzstan. Situated in the northern Tien Shan ("Celestial Mountains"), it is one of the largest high-mountain lakes in the world and is famous for its magnificent scenery and unique scientific interest. It is situated within the bottom edges of the Lake Ysyk basin, which is bordered to the north by the Kungöy Ala Range and to the south by the Teskey Ala Range. The lake has a length of 182 km (113 miles), a width up to 61 km (38 miles), and a surface area of 6,280 square km (2,425 square miles). It reaches a depth of 668 metres (2,192 feet) and averages some 280 metres (920 feet) deep. The lake's Kyrgyz name, Ysyk-köl, means "Hot Lake," alluding to the fact that it does not freeze over during the winter.

The Kungöy Ala Range (with elevations up to 4,771 metres [15,653 feet]) and the Teskey Ala (up to 5,216 metres [17,113 feet]) frame the Lake Ysyk basin with steep slopes and rocky crests. The basin's climate is warm, dry, and temperate. Air temperatures in July on the shore average about 17 °C (62 °F); in January, on the western edge of the basin, the temperatures average about -2 °C (28 °F). The annual amount of precipitation increases sharply from west to east, from 100 mm (4 inches) to a maximum of 410 to 510 mm (16 to 20 inches) in summer. Strong winds blow frequently toward the lake, with velocities in the west reaching some 105 to 145 km (65 to 90 miles) per hour.

More than 50 streams and short rivers are found in the basin. The largest, the Dzhergalan and the Tyup, are each nearly 97 km (60 miles) long and are located in the eastern part of the basin. The Chu River flows along the western outskirts of the basin.

Lake Ysyk's shores open out gently, with coves on the eastern and southeastern sides. Sandy soils predominate. The water of the lake is sky blue in colour, clear (visibility down to 20 metres [65 feet]), and moderately salty. Although the salinity makes its waters unsuitable for drinking and irrigation, it is possible to use them without freshening for watering cattle.

Rocky deserts with sparse, saline, semi-bushy vegetation lie in the western part of the basin. Toward the east are steppes and meadows and a type of elm that grows in the chestnut soils and black earth. Higher up in the mountains are found subalpine and alpine meadows.

Some two dozen kinds of fish live in Lake Ysyk, including such endemic species as the Issyk-kul marinka (*Schizothorax pseudoaksaiensis issykkuli*), the Issyk-kul chebachok (*Leuciscus bergi*), and the endangered naked osman (*Gymnodiptchus dybowskii*). Among the species of commercial fish are common carp and whitefish, the latter introduced into the lake.

The lake's western and eastern shores serve as a wintering place for waterfowl. Pochards, mallards, bald coots, and teals are the main varieties. To conserve the wildlife, the Issyk-Kul Preserve (now National Preserve) was founded in 1948, encompassing a lake waterfront and a 1.6-km (1-mile) shore zone in which hunting is forbidden. Hare, fox, and muskrat live in the thickets. In all there are some 40 kinds of mammals and 200 types of birds. A much larger area was designated a UNESCO biosphere reserve in 2001, the intention being to correct or reverse some of the cumulative environmental degradation caused by human occupation and use in the region.

The basin's population consists largely of Kyrgyz, but there are also a number of Russians, Ukrainians, Tatars, Uzbeks, and Dungans. There are two large cities—Karakol (Przhevalsk) and Balykchy (Issyk-Kul)—and hundreds of villages. The principal occupation in the area is farming: wheat, potatoes, and vegetables are grown and livestock raised. The shores of the lake are noted for their health resorts.

TONLE SAP

Tonle Sap (Khmer: Bœng Tônlé Sab) is a natural flood-plain reservoir in central Cambodia. The lake is drained during the dry season by the Sab River (Tônlé Sab) across the Véal Pôc plain southeastward to the Mekong River. Called by the French Grand Lac ("Great Lake"), the lake is fed by numerous erratic tributaries and also by the Srêng and Sên rivers, which are perennial northern tributaries. During the June-to-November monsoonal regime, the swollen Mekong reverses the southeastward flow of the Sab River, which increases Tonle Sap's area from about 2,700 square km (1,050 square miles) to about 10,360 square km (4,000 square miles); its depth also increases from 0.9–3 metres (3–10 feet) to 9–14 metres (30–45 feet), permitting vessels with 3 metres (9 feet) of draft to navigate it up through the various tributaries, on which are situated the towns of Kâmpóng Thum (Kompong Thom), Siĕmréab, Bătdâmbâng (Battambang), and Poŭthĭsăt (Pursat). During the rainy season the lake's width increases from about 35 km (22 miles) to 105 km (65 miles). At low water it is little more than a reed-infested swamp, with channels for fishing craft.

The lake, the largest freshwater body in Southeast Asia, supports a large carp-breeding and carp-harvesting industry, with numerous floating fishing villages inhabited largely by ethnic Vietnamese. The fermented and salted fish are staples of the Cambodian diet. UNESCO designated Tonle Sap a biosphere reserve in 1997.

APPENDIX B
AVERAGE NET PRIMARY PRODUCTION OF THE EARTH'S MAJOR HABITATS

AVERAGE NET PRIMARY PRODUCTION OF THE EARTH'S MAJOR HABITATS	
HABITAT	NET PRIMARY PRODUCTION (GRAM PER SQUARE METRE PER YEAR)
Forests	
tropical	1,800
temperate	1,250
boreal	800
Other Terrestrial Habitats	
swamp and marsh	2,500
savanna	700
cultivated land	650
shrubland	600
desert scrub	70
temperate grassland	500
tundra and alpine	140
Aquatic Habitats	
algal beds and reefs	2,000
estuaries	1,800
lakes and streams	500
continental shelf	360
open ocean	125

Source: Adapted from Robert E. Ricklefs, *Ecology*, 3rd edition (1990), by W.H. Freeman and Company, used with permission.

AREAS AND VOLUMES OF THE GREAT LAKES						
	SURFACE AREA		WORLD RANK	VOLUME		WORLD RANK
	SQ MI	SQ KM		CU MI	CU KM	
Superior	31,700	82,100	2nd	2,900	12,100	4th
Michigan	22,300	57,800	5th	1,180	4,920	6th
Huron	23,000	59,600	4th	850	3,540	7th
Erie	9,910	25,670	11th	116	484	15th
Ontario	7,340	19,010	14th	393	1,640	11th

GLOSSARY

aphotic zone The dark, bottom zone, or layer, of a body of water

bathymetry The measurement of ocean depth

ectogenic Of or pertaining to the capability of development apart from a host, used chiefly of pathogenic bacteria.

endorheic A drainage system wherein surface waters drain to inland termini, such as permanent or temporary lakes, where they eventually evaporate or seep away; also known as a "closed system."

eutrophication The process by which a body of water becomes enriched with dissolved nutrients that stimulate the growth of aquatic plant life, usually resulting in the depletion of dissolved oxygen.

evaporites Any of a variety of individual minerals found in the sedimentary deposit of soluble salts that results from the evaporation of water.

exorheic A drainage system characterized by surface waters that ultimately drain to the ocean in well-defined patterns that involve streams and rivers temporarily impounded by permanent freshwater lakes.

graben A depressed segment of the crust of the earth or a celestial body (as the moon) bounded on at least two sides by faults.

holomictic Characterized by circulation of waters from the top to the bottom.

hypolimnion The lower strata of lake water, having a temperature that uniform throughout the strata yet typically cooler than that of the lake's other levels.

Langmuir circulation The relatively organized mixing mechanism wherein sinking occurs at surface streaks created by the wind, and upwelling occurs between the streaks.

lentic Of, relating to, or living in still waters such as those in lakes.

limnology A subdiscipline of hydrology that concerns the study of fresh waters such as lakes, including their biological, physical, and chemical aspects.

lotic Of, relating to, or living in actively moving water.

meromictic Lake waters that do not completely circulate, leaving them stratified.

moraine An accumulation of rock debris (till) carried or deposited by a glacier.

névé Granular snow adjacent to glacier ice

oligotrophic A condition pertaining to lake waters that are poorly fed by the nutrients nitrogen and phosphorus, and have low concentrations of these constituents.

piedmont A district lying along the foot of a mountain range.

plankton Marine and freshwater organisms that, because they are unable to move or are too small or too weak to swim against water currents, exist in a drifting, floating state.

seiche An oscillatory wave of long period.

tectonic Relating to changes to the structure of Earth's crust or the surface of another celestial body.

thermocline A layer in a thermally stratified body of water that separates an upper, warmer, lighter region from a lower, colder, heavier one.

BIBLIOGRAPHY

INLAND WATER ECOSYSTEMS

G. Evelyn Hutchinson, *A Treatise on Limnology*, 4 vol. (1957–93), provides essential reading for anyone interested in a serious study of inland waters. Robert G. Wetzel, *Limnology*, 2nd ed. (1983), is a basic and thorough text on the major limnological features of lakes. Mary J. Burgis and Pat Morris, *The Natural History of Lakes* (1987), presents global coverage. Jürgen Schwoerbel, *Handbook of Limnology* (1987; originally published in German, 1984), is a comprehensive treatment. R. Margalef (ed.), *Limnology Now: A Paradigm of Planetary Problems* (1994), discusses many subjects of direct relevance to the importance of inland waters within the biosphere. Gerald A. Cole, *Textbook of Limnology*, 4th ed. (1994), explains many of the physicochemical events associated with inland waters. Lake Biwa Research Institute and International Lake Environment Committee (eds.), *Data Book of World Lake Environments: A Survey of the State of World Lakes*, 2 vol. (1987–89), looks at the physicochemical and biological features of many of the world's lakes. U. Theodore Hammer, *Saline Lake Ecosystems of the World* (1986), offers a full account of inland saline ecosystems. H.B.N. Hynes, *The Ecology of Running Waters* (1970), although dated, is a classic text and still an excellent guide. William A. Niering, *Wetlands* (1985), introduces the major types of water found in North America and their biota. Brian Moss, *Ecology of Fresh Waters*, 2nd ed. (1988), explores the ecology of freshwater lakes and rivers. R.S.K. Barnes and K.h. Mann (eds.), *Fundamentals of Aquatic Ecology*, 2nd ed. (1991), contains several relevant essays on inland waters. Max Finlayson and Michael Moser (eds.), *Wetlands* (1991), deals with all inland waters of the world from a conservation perspective. National Research Council (U.S.), Committee on Restoration of Aquatic Ecosystems—Science, Technology, and Public Policy, *Restoration of Aquatic Ecosystems: Science, Technology, and Public Policy* (1992), discusses how to restore to natural or near-natural conditions inland waters that have been altered by human abuse.

LAKES

Mary J. Burgis and Pat Morris, *The Natural History of Lakes* (1987); and Laurence Pringle et al., *Rivers and Lakes* (1985), are two treatments written for the general reader. Less fundamental but more recent summaries of scientific lake studies include Gerald A. Cole, *Textbook of Limnology*, 4th ed. (1994); Charles R. Goldman and Alexander J. Horne, *Limnology* (1983); Robert G. Wetzel, *Limnology*, 2nd ed. (1983); Abraham Lerman (ed.), *Lakes—Chemistry, Geology, Physics* (1978); and Werner Stumm (ed.), *Chemical Processes in Lakes* (1985). Up-to-date books on hydrology and hydrogeology are R. Allan Freeze and John A. Cherry, *Groundwater* (1979); Patrick A. Domenico and Franklin W. Schwartz, *Physical and Chemical Hydrogeology* (1990); and Rafael L. Bras, *Hydrology* (1990). The sedimentology of lakes is the subject of J. McManus and R.W. Duck (eds.), *Geomorphology and Sedimentology of Lakes and Reservoirs* (1993). Prediction of the behaviour of lakes is dealt with in B. Henderson-Sellers, *Engineering Limnology* (1984); and A. James (ed.), *An Introduction to Water Quality Modelling*, 2nd ed. (1993). The dynamics of lakes are covered by K. Hutter (ed.), *Hydrodynamics of Lakes* (1984); James Lighthill, *Waves in Fluids* (1978); and Jerome Williams and Samuel A. Elder, *Fluid Physics for Oceanographers and Physicists* (1989). An up-to-date book on general freshwater biology is Brian Moss, *Ecology of Fresh Waters*, 2nd ed. (1988). Also of interest on this subject are the studies by C.S. Reynolds, *The Ecology of Freshwater Phytoplankton* (1984); and by Max M. Tilzer and Colette Serruya (eds.), *Large Lakes: Ecological Structure and Function* (1990). The consequences of building large-scale dams are analyzed in Edward Goldsmith and Nicholas Hildyard, *The Social and Environmental Effects of Large Dams* (1986). Kent W. Thornton, Bruce L. Kimmel, and Forrest E. Payne (eds.), *Reservoir Limnology* (1990), analyzes the ecology of reservoirs in their similarities to and differences from lakes. The effects of pollution on lakes are discussed in B. Henderson-Sellers and H.R. Markland, *Decaying Lakes: The Origins and Control of Cultural Eutrophication* (1987); E.B. Welch and T. Lindell, *Ecological Effects of Wastewater: Applied Limnology and Pollution Effects* (1992); Theodora E. Colborn et al., *Great Lakes, Great Legacy?* (1990); and William Ashworth, *The Late, Great Lakes: An Environmental History* (1986). Continuing research can be found in *Limnology and Oceanography* (bimonthly).

CASPIAN SEA

A.N. Kosarev and E.A. Yablonskaya, *The Caspian Sea* (1994), provides an overview of the sea. A useful map of the Caspian region is National Geographic Society, *Caspian Region: Promise and Peril* (1999). For a review of scientific, environmental, and political issues, see Iwao Kobori and Michael H. Glantz (eds.), *Central Eurasian Water Crisis* (1998); and Michael H. Glantz and Igor S. Zonn, *Scientific, Environmental, and Political Issues in the Circum-Caspian Region* (1997). Russian scientific treatments include A.N. Kosarev, *Gidrologiia Kaspiĭskogo i Aral'skogo moreĭ* (1975), a study of the hydrology of the

Caspian and Aral seas; S.S. Baĭdin and A.N. Kosarev (eds.), *Kaspiĭskoe more: gidrologiia i gidrokhimiia* (1986), an analysis of hydrology and chemistry of the Caspian Sea; and N.A. Krylov (ed.), *Kaspiĭskoe more: geologiia i neftegazonosnost'* (1987), a survey of submarine geology focusing on the Caspian gas and oil resources. English-language research findings on the sea include V.A. Vronskiy, "The Holocene Stratigraphy and Paleogeography of the Caspian Sea," *International Geology Review*, 29(1):14–24 (1987); and Yu.A. Karpychev, "Fluctuations of the Caspian Sea Level as an Indicator of Global Climatic Changes," *Nuclear Geophysics*, 4(1):57–70 (1990).

THE GREAT LAKES

A thorough, scientifically advanced treatise on the geologic evolution of the Great Lakes, focusing on glaciation, is provided in P.F. Karrow and P.E. Calkin, *Quaternary Evolution of the Great Lakes* (1984). Harlan Hatcher and Erich A. Walter, *A Pictorial History of the Great Lakes* (1963), surveys early exploration, shipping, and settlement in the region. Useful background information on the region is found in Lee Botts et al., *The Great Lakes: An Environmental Atlas and Resource Book* (1987); and R.A. Assel et al., *Great Lakes Ice Atlas* (1983). A history of ecological changes in the basin and their effect on the lakes is presented in William Ashworth, *The Late, Great Lakes* (1986). Theodora E. Colborn et al., *Great Lakes, Great Legacy?* (1990), discusses the Great Lakes as an ecosystem, changes in the lakes' environment, and institutional arrangements for dealing with these problems. The region's economic situation is assessed in Federal Reserve Bank of Chicago and Great Lakes Commission, *The Great Lakes Economy* (1985), a compendium of data on resources and industry, and *The Great*

Lakes Economy: Looking North and South (1991), an interpretive analysis. Noel M. Burns, *Erie: The Lake That Survived* (1985), discusses the environmental and economic degradation of the lake and its environs and the signs of rehabilitation. Also useful is Great Lakes Science Advisory Board, *Report* (biennial), which includes summaries of health, societal, and education issues related to pollution and toxic chemicals.

LAKE CHAD

Jean Maley, "Histoire de la végétation et du climat de l'Afrique nord-tropicale au Quaternaire récent," *Bothalia*, 14(3–4):377–389 (September 1983), presents a long-term view of climate change in the Chad basin. J.-P. Carmouze, J.-R. Durand, and C. Lévêque (eds.), *Lake Chad: Ecology and Productivity of a Shallow Tropical Ecosystem* (1983), is a lengthy study of the lake's environment and productivity. The fish of Lake Chad and its tributaries are described in J. Blache and F. Miton, *Les Poissons du bassin du Tchad et du bassin adjacent du Mayo Kebbi* (1964). A particularly useful study of the peoples of the Chad basin is Albert Le Rouvreur, *Sahéliens et Sahariens du Tchad* (1962, reissued 1989). The more recently arrived Arab groups are discussed in J.C. Zeltner, *Les Arabes dans la région du Lac Tchad: problèmes d'origine et de chronologie* (1977).

WETLANDS

Donald S. McLusky, *The Estuarine Ecosystem,* 2nd ed. (1989), is a concise account of the subject at the college level. John W. Day, Jr., et al., *Estuarine Ecology* (1989), deals with physical aspects, plants, animals, organic detritus, and human impacts, including some information on lagoons. K.H. Mann, *Ecology of Coastal Waters: A Systems*

Approach (1982), discusses estuaries as well as sea grass, marsh grass, mangrove, seaweed, and mudflat communities. S.P. Long and C.F. Mason, *Saltmarsh Ecology* (1983), treats such topics as the formation, flora, fauna, physiography, and conservation of salt marshes. J.R. Lewis, *The Ecology of Rocky Shores* (1964), is still a standard work on organisms and their relationship to the environment. Roger N. Brehaut, *Ecology of Rocky Shores* (1982), is a concise, nontechnical text with suggestions for further reading. A.C. Brown and A. McLachlan, *Ecology of Sandy Shores* (1990), discusses sandy beaches worldwide. John R. Clark, *Coastal Ecosystems: Ecological Considerations for Management of the Coastal Zone* (1974), and *Coastal Ecosystem Management: A Technical Manual for the Conservation of Coastal Zone Resources* (1977, reprinted 1983), discuss the ecology of marine boundary ecosystems and the problems of management.

Patrick Dugan (ed.), *Wetlands in Danger: A World Conservation Atlas* (1993), summarizes all the world's major wetlands and wetland types. William J. Mitsch and James G. Gosselink, *Wetlands*, 2nd ed. (1993), describes seven major types of wetlands and the principles common to all wetlands. William A. Niering, *Wetlands* (1985), an illustrated text, details the habitats' features and characteristics. William J. Mitsch (ed.), *Global Wetlands: Old World and New* (1994), covers topics such as the biogeochemistry, modeling, and ecological engineering of wetlands, as well as wildlife management and river delta management. Regional accounts can be found in Canada Committee on Ecological (Biophysical) Land Classification, National Wetlands Working Group, *Wetlands of Canada* (1988), including an extensive bibliography; A.J. McComb and P.S. Lake, *Australian Wetlands* (1990); and Bates Littlehales and William A. Niering, *Wetlands of North America* (1991), both heavily illustrated with photographs. Edward Maltby, *Waterlogged Wealth: Why Waste the World's Wet Places?* (1986), describes the functions of wetlands and the degree to which they are threatened around the world. Jon A. Kusler, William J. Mitsch, and Joseph S. Larson, "Wetlands," *Scientific American*, 270(1):64–70 (January 1994), summarizes the structure and function of wetlands, emphasizing the importance of a fluctuating water level on ecosystem function. Dennis Whigham, Dagmar Dykyjová, and Slavomil Hejný (eds.), *Wetlands of the World: Inventory, Ecology, and Management* (1993–), is a scholarly treatment. Max Finlayson and Michael Moser (eds.), *Wetlands* (1991), deals with all inland waters of the world from a conservation perspective.

THE EVERGLADES

Marjory Stoneman Douglas, *The Everglades: River of Grass*, rev. ed. (1988), is a well-written and well-documented volume. David McCally, *The Everglades: An Environmental History* (1999), covers the area's development from its geologic origins to 20th-century agriculture. Glen Simmons and Laura Ogden, *Gladesmen: Gator Hunters, Moonshiners, and Skiffers* (1998), provides a portrait of life in the Everglades in the 1930s.

INDEX

A

Abert Lake, 10
adaptations, biota, 74–75,
    123, 133, 141, 152, 153,
    157, 158
äfja, 21
Africa, 1, 3, 10, 11, 55, 119
Agassiz, Lake, 109, 131
Agassiz, Louis, 109
Alaska, 2, 17, 147
Albemarle Sound, 168
Albert, Lake, 61
Alberta, 2, 112
algae, 36, 73, 74, 75, 78, 94,
    134, 138, 141, 143, 153, 177
algal zonation, 142
Allouez, Claude-Jean,
    103, 108
Amu Darya, 3
anaerobic conditions, 7, 27
Angara River, 113, 114
animal life, 94, 95, 103, 112,
    114–115, 118, 123–124,
    126–127, 128, 129, 134,
    135–137, 138, 140, 141–
    142, 142–143, 143–144,
    145, 146, 152, 153, 162,
    163, 166–167, 169, 170,
    173, 174, 176–177
anoxic conditions, 26, 27,
    28, 152, 172

Antarctica, 34, 71
Antelope Island, 111, 112
aphotic zone, 5
Aqaba, Gulf of, 82
Aqsū River, 117
aquatic ecosystems, 71, 73,
    132, 151–152
aquatic productivity,
    77–79
Aral Sea, 2–3, 10, 72, 116, 178
Arctic Circle, 95
Arctic Ocean, 90, 94, 112
arheic systems, 65
Asia, 8, 11, 13, 77, 80, 143,
    151, 160
Astor, John Jacob, 108
Aswan High Dam, 130
Athabaska, Lake, 14
Atlantic Intracoast
    Waterway, 168
Atlantic Ocean, 14–15, 22,
    97, 120, 143, 172
Australia, 10, 22, 61, 77,
    140, 143
Ayaguz Lake, 117
Azov, Sea of, 87

B

bacteriological contamina-
    tion, 40
Baikal, Lake, 1, 11, 34, 49, 59,
    66, 80, 96, 113–116, 127

Balkhash, Lake, 80, 116–119
Bangweulu, 163
Barents Sea, 90
Barguzin River, 113, 114
Barisan Mountains, 12
basins, 1, 3, 7–23, 81, 111, 116, 119
basin topography, 17–19
beaches, 47, 50, 110, 143–144
Bear Lake, 110
Bear River, 109, 112
Beaver Island, 101
Belgium, 30, 36
benthos zone, 50, 76–77
Benue River, 120
Big Cypress Swamp, 163–164, 165
Big Soda Lake, 27
biogenic meromixis, 32
biological oxygen demand (BOD), 26
biological productivity, 4, 13, 25, 28, 29, 77–79
biomass production, 4, 78, 176
biospheres, 64, 68, 70, 71, 75, 79, 164
bitter lakes, 22
Black Island, 131
Black River, 104
Black Sea, 10, 87, 90
Boccaro, Caspar, 126
BOD (biological oxygen demand), 26

bogs, 130, 144, 145, 146–147, 151, 153–155, 170, 173, 174
Bonneville, Lake, 10–11, 110, 111
Bonney, Lake, 34
Boteti River, 171
bottom morphology, 42, 51, 52
boundary ecosystems, 130, 132, 150, 151–152
Bridger, Jim, 111
British Columbia, 14, 140
Brûlé, Étienne, 98, 100, 104–105, 108
Burton, Sir Richard, 128
Byrd, William, 168

C

calderas, 12
California, 8, 10, 22, 140
Cameroon River, 119, 125
Canada, 2, 13, 14, 95, 96, 97, 100, 109, 112, 113, 140, 144, 147, 148
capillary waves, 46
Caprivi Strip, 171
carbon dioxide, 22, 26–27, 68
Caspian Sea, 1–2, 10, 61, 71, 80, 86–95
Cattaraugus Creek, 97
Cayuga, Lake, 49
Central Asia, 1, 2–3, 72, 86, 178
Chad, Lake, 119–126

Chad basin, 3, 120
Chad River, 119
Chambeshi River, 163
Champlain, Lake, 10
Champlain, Samuel de, 100, 104
Chari River, 121–122
chemical oxygen demand (COD), 26
chemical pollution, 39, 40
chemical precipitation, 19, 21–23, 27
Chesapeake Bay, 138, 168
Chicago, 102, 103, 150
Chicago River, 101
Chikoy River, 113
China, 148, 150, 151, 175–176
Chobe River, 172
cirques, 14
clastic sediments, 19, 20–21
clays, 19, 20, 21, 82
clinogrades, 62
closed basins, 171
closed lakes, 3, 56
coastal ecosystems, 135
coastal mudflats, 132
coastal systems, 132–144
Coldwater Ditch, 168
Columbia River, 59, 110
common mangroves, 159–162
Congaree National Park, 164
consumers, 75, 142, 145
Coriolis force, 43–44, 45
Crater Lake, 12

Cree Indians, 131, 208
crenogenic meromixis, 32
cultural eutrophication, 29–30
currents, 5, 6, 16–17, 18–19, 20, 21, 24, 33, 36, 42–46, 50–52, 94, 101, 104, 132, 136
Cuyahoga River, 97
cyanobacteria, 30, 75, 78, 94

D

Dalton's formula, 57
dams, 10–11, 13, 15–16, 16–17, 51–52, 53–54, 59, 94, 130, 144
Dead Sea, 71, 80–86, 110
decomposers, 75, 76
Deep Creek, 168
Deep Lake, 16
Deer Island, 131
deltas, 51, 114, 129, 170, 171–172, 175
denivellations, 44, 48, 49
Detroit River, 97, 99
diatoms, 30, 94
Diefenbaker, Lake, 51–52
Djourab Depression, 120
drainage systems, 65, 71
dredging, 18–19, 23, 50, 53, 59, 98
Drummond, Lake, 168–169
DuLhut, Daniel Greysolon, sieur, 108

E

Earn, Loch, 49
East African rift system,
126, 127, 129
Ebeji River, 122
ecology, wetland, 151–152
ecosystems, 23, 64–79, 130,
132, 135, 144, 145, 149–
150, 151–152, 172, 176
ectogenic meromixis, 32
Eifel, Germany, 12
Elizabeth River, 168
Ellesmere Island, 34
Emin Pasha Gulf, 130
endangered species habi-
tats, 164, 167
endorheic drainage sys-
tems, 65, 71
energy balance, 6
English Lake District, 14, 21
epilimnion, 5, 32, 35, 45,
49–50, 68
Erie, Lake, 6, 17, 25, 97–98,
99, 100, 103, 104
Erie Indians, 99
erosion, 5, 7, 17, 18–19, 20,
23, 24, 42, 50–51, 52, 53,
62, 66, 88
estuaries, 30, 135, 136, 137,
159, 162, 166, 175
Euphrates River, 170
eutrophication, 4, 29–30,
40, 78, 79

evaporation, 34, 35, 42,
53–54, 56–57, 58–59, 64,
71, 82, 83, 93, 109, 120–
121, 122, 174
evaporites, 8
evapotranspiration, 55, 146
Everglades, 145, 163, 164,
165–167
exorheic regions, 65
explorations, 94–95,
98–99, 100, 103, 104,
110–111, 112, 125, 126,
128, 130, 131
extinction, lake, 62–63

F

Feeder Ditch, 169
fens, 147–148
fetch, 46
Finger Lakes, 13, 15–16
fjords, 14
floodplains, 146
Florida, 10, 16, 165
Florida Bay, 165, 166
fluvial processes, 16–17
forested swamps, 149
förna, 21
Fox River, 101
Frémont, John C., 111
freshwater lakes, 1, 66,
75–76, 76–77, 79, 162
freshwater tidal marshes,
130, 132, 137–138, 144, 145
freshwater wetlands, 146, 153

G

Garda, Lake, 49
Garstin, Sir William, 130
Genesee River, 104
Geneva, Lake, 48–49
George, Lake, 61
giant kelps, 138–140
glacial activities, 1, 8,
    13–16, 19, 21, 59, 91,
    109, 110, 147
grabens, 1, 11, 81, 82
gradient currents, 44
gradients, 26, 31, 32, 33, 35,
    42–44, 48, 56–57, 69
Grand River, 97, 101
grasses, 1, 123, 132, 135, 136,
    142–143, 145, 146, 147,
    153, 155, 163, 165, 166,
    172, 174, 176
Great Barrier Reef, 143
Great Basin region, 10,
    111
Great Bear Lake, 95–96
Great Bear River, 96
Great Dismal Swamp,
    167–169
Great Lakes, 1, 14, 37, 59, 66,
    80, 96–108, 147
Great Lakes–St. Lawrence
    Seaway, 102
Great Rann, 137
Great Salt Lake, 10,
    109–112

Great Slave Lake, 14, 112
Green Bay, 101, 103
groundwater, 1, 2, 16, 33, 42,
    53, 54, 55–56, 65, 122,
    146–147, 149, 155
gyttja, 21

H

halophytes, 85, 133
Ḥammār, Lake, 170, 171
Hearne, Samuel, 112
heat budgets, 32–35
heaths, 153, 154
heat transfer, 34, 35–37
Hecla Island, 131
Hefner, Lake, 34–35, 57, 59
Hemmelsdorfersee, 32
Highveld, 70
Himmerland, 169–170
holomictic lakes, 31, 32
Hornborgasjön, Lake, 23
Hudson Bay, 109
Hudson River, 131
human activities, 4, 8, 17,
    23–24, 29, 51–52, 73, 87,
    138, 150–151, 174,
    177–178
Huron, Lake, 61, 96, 97, 98,
    99–101, 104, 105
Huron Indians, 100, 101
Huron River, 97
Hutchinson, G.E., 8
hydraulic effects, 42–43
hydraulic gradients, 42

hydrologic cycle, 1, 2, 3,
    52–63, 64, 65, 71, 87, 95,
    117, 119, 145, 150
hydrophytes, 145
hypolimnion, 5, 32, 35, 36,
    45, 49–50, 63, 68

I

Iceland, 12–13
ice-scour lakes, 13–14
ice sheets, 1, 13–16, 21, 109
Ile River, 117, 118
inflows, 5, 6, 8, 20, 24, 33, 42,
    44, 51, 54, 55, 59, 62, 71,
    83, 93, 99, 109, 110, 114,
    117, 121–122, 146–147
inland water ecosystems,
    75–79, 144
inland water origins, 64–66
inland wetland systems,
    144–150
internal seiches, 45
internal waves, 45–46
International Union for
    Conservation of
    Nature and Natural
    Resources, 178
Iroquois Indians, 98, 100,
    104–105
islands, 12, 14, 34, 72, 87, 89,
    95, 97, 99, 100–101, 104,
    106–107, 111, 112, 121,
    122, 126, 127, 130, 131,
    163, 166, 172, 173, 175
Italy, 12, 49

J

Jolliet, Louis, 98, 100
Jordan River, 83, 109, 112

K

Kachchh, Gulf of, 137
Kagera River, 129, 130
Kalamazoo River, 101
Kalambo River, 127–128
Kaministikwia River, 106
Kanem, 120, 122, 123, 125
Kara-Bogaz-Gol, 88
karstic phenomena, 16
Katonga River, 130
Kavirondo Gulf, 129–130
kelps, 138–140
Kendyrli-Kayasansk, 88
kettle lakes, 16
Kiira dam, 130
Kioga, Lake, 10
Knipovich, Nikolai M., 95
Kura River, 88
Kwania, Lake, 10

L

*Lake of the Dismal Swamp,
    The*, 169
lakes
    basins, 7–23, 42, 51, 62
    chemical composition of,
        23–28
    commercial usage of,
        37–38, 85, 96–97, 98,
        99–100, 102–103,

107–108, 111, 112, 115–116, 118, 119, 124, 127, 131, 150–151, 153, 177–178
currents of, 43–44
ecosystems of, 23
extinctions, 62–63
hydrologic balances of, 52–63
nutrients, 28, 29, 79
sounding of, 5, 17
usages of, 37–39
land reclamation, 174–175, 176
Langmuir circulation, 45–46
La Salle, Robert Cavelier, sieur de, 100, 103
Laurentide Ice Sheet, 109
lava formations, 12–13
lentic systems, 65–66
Lepsi River, 117
Likoma Island, 126, 127
limnology, 3–7
Lisān, Al-, 73, 80, 82, 83
Little Rann of Kachchh, 137
littoral zones, 50, 62, 63
Livingstone, David, 126, 129, 163
Logone River, 121–122
long-wave radiation, 6, 32–33, 34, 35
lotic systems, 66
Lualaba River, 128
Luapula River, 163
Lukuga River, 128
Lünersee, 16

M

maars, 12
Mackenzie River, 96, 112
Mackinac Island, 100–101
Mackinac, Straits of, 99, 101
Ma‘dan, 170
Makgadikgadi Pans, 171
Malagarasi River, 127
Malawi, Lake, 126
management, wetlands, 150–151
mangroves, 130, 132, 133–134, 151, 158–162, 165, 166, 175
Manistee River, 101, 103
Manitoulin Island, 99
Mansfeldersee, 16
Marquette, Jacques, 100, 103
Marsh Arabs, 170
marshes, 63, 130, 132, 155–157, 173
Mary, Lake, 32
Maumee River, 97
Mead, Lake, 59
Mediterranean Sea, 87
Mega-Chad, 119
Mendota, Lake, 59
Menominee River, 101
meromictic lakes, 26, 31, 34
meromixis, 31–32
mesotrophic lakes, 79
mesotrophy, 62
metalimnion, 68
meteorite craters, 17–18

Mexico, Gulf of, 159, 165
Miccosukee Indians, 164
Michigan, 32, 61, 96, 97, 99, 100, 101, 105, 107
Michigan, Lake, 96, 98, 99, 101–103
Minnesota, 14, 97, 105, 109
Minnesota River, 109
mires, 146
Mississippi River, 59, 109
Molopo River, 172
Moore, Thomas, 169
moors, 146
moraines, glacial, 13, 15–16
morphology, bottom, 42, 51, 52
Moses Lake, 17
mudflats, 111, 112, 132, 137, 143–144, 145, 155
Muskegon River, 101
Mývatyn, Lake, 12–13

N

Nalubaale Dam, 130
Nasser, Lake, 5
Nata River, 171–172
Native Americans, 98, 99, 100, 101, 103, 104–105, 112, 131, 164, 173
Nelson River, 131
Netherlands, 30
neuston, 76–77
Nevada, 27, 32
Newfoundland Evaporation Basin, 111

New York, 13, 15–16, 49, 97, 98, 104
New Zealand, 12
Niagara River, 97, 104
Nicolet, Jean, 103
Nigeria River, 119
nitrates, 8, 22, 23, 27, 40
nontidal freshwater systems, 145
North American Great Lakes, 14, 38
North American Waterfowl Management Plan, 151
North Sea, 30
Norway, 14, 16
Nova Scotia, 17, 140
Nyasa, Lake, 61, 126–127

O

Okavango Delta, 171–172
Okavango River, 171
Okeechobee, Lake, 10, 166
Okefenokee Swamp, 172–173
Oklahoma, 34–35
oligotrophic waters, 29, 62–63, 78
Ontario, Lake, 34–35, 43, 58–59, 61, 98, 103–105,
open lakes, 56
open wetland systems, 147
Orange River, 172
Oregon, 10, 12
orthophosphates, 23, 27–28

Oswego River, 104
outflows, 3, 6, 16, 20, 33, 42, 53, 59, 61, 62, 93, 110, 114, 147
overturns, 5, 31–32, 68
Owen Falls Dam, 130
oxygen, 7, 25–26, 29, 40, 62–63, 68–69, 73, 74, 134, 177

P

Pacific Ocean, 110, 138
Padma River, 175
Paine, Robert, 142
paleolimnology, 19
Pangong Lake, 61
Pantanal, 146
Paraguay River, 146
Pasquotank River, 168
Pearlette ash deposit, 21
peat, 14, 19, 61, 133, 141, 146–148, 151, 155, 166, 170, 176
Pelee Island, 97
Pere Marquette River, 101
permanent waters, 66–70, 72–73
Perry, Oliver H., 99
Peter I the Great, 94
phosphates, 27–28, 40, 78
photic zones, 75–76
photosynthesis, 5, 22, 25, 26, 29, 75–76, 78
pH values, 7, 22, 26, 27, 145, 147
phytoplankton, 4, 5, 28, 30, 76–77

Pic River, 106
piedmont lakes, 14
Pigeon River, 106
Pinsk Marshes, 174
plankton, 29, 36, 75, 76–77, 134, 135, 141
plant life, 85, 114–115, 118, 122, 123, 128, 133, 135, 136, 137, 138–140, 142–143, 147, 152, 153–162, 163, 164, 166, 170, 172–173, 174, 176–177
pollution, 4, 20, 24, 36, 38, 39, 40, 96–97, 98, 103, 115–116, 118, 177
ponds, 3–4, 63
Portage River, 97
Precambrian African Shield, 120
precipitation, 27, 32, 33, 41, 42, 53, 54–55, 59, 61, 71, 82, 92, 93, 118, 120, 121, 144–145, 146, 173–174
pressure gradients, 42–44, 48, 56–57
primary production, 75–76, 77–78, 79, 176
Pripet Marshes, 173–175
Pripet River, 173
Provost, Étienne, 111

Q

Qaratal River, 117
Quebec, 17
Quetico, 14

R

Radisson, Pierre Espirit, 108
raised bogs, 153, 155
Raisin River, 97
Rann of Kachchh, 137
Rasmar Convention, 151
Red River, 109, 131
Red Sea, 11
riparian ecosystems, 144–145,
    149–150
Rocky Mountains, 17
Ruhuhu River, 126
Russia, 34
Russian Platform, 90
Ruzizi River, 127

S

salinity, 69, 71, 72–73, 83–85,
    94, 110, 114, 117, 118,
    133–134, 135, 137, 153
salinity gradients, 26, 31,
    32, 69
salt lakes, 10, 24, 72, 80,
    109–112
salt marsh ecosystems,
    135–136
salt marshes, 130, 132, 134–137,
    137–138, 151, 159
Salt Sea, 80
salt swamps, 158–162, 175
saltwater estuaries, 162
Samur River, 88
sand dunes, 102

sand flats, 143–144
sand spits, 136
Sandusky River, 97
São Lourenço River, 146
Sārez, Lake, 13
Saskatachewan, 51–52
Saskatchewan River, 109, 131
saw grass, 145, 165, 166
Saxony, 16
Scheldt, 30
scouring, glacier, 13–14,
    15–16, 147
sea grass, 132, 142–143, 166
seaweeds, 133, 138–140,
    141–142, 143
secondary production, 78, 79
sedges, 145, 147, 153, 155, 158
sediments, 4, 5, 16–17,
    18–19, 19–23, 51, 53, 63,
    82, 91, 114, 122, 132, 134,
    135, 143, 146
Sedom, 83
Sedom, Mount, 82, 85
seepage, 121
Seewlisee, 16
seiches, 6, 42, 45, 48–50, 92
Selenga River, 113
Seminole Indians, 164, 173
sensible heat, 33, 34
settlements, early, 81, 90,
    98–99, 100–101, 103,
    104–105, 111, 125
shingle spits, 136
Shire River, 126

shoreline ecosystems, 132
shortwave radiation, 6
Sierra Nevada, 10, 13
silica, 12, 28, 30
silts, 20, 109, 127, 136, 137, 142
Silver Lake, 17
Snake River, 110
Soda Lake, 32
Sodon Lake, 32
Soimonov, Fedor I., 94
solar radiation, 32, 33, 34, 35
Songpan Grasslands, 176
sounding, lake, 5, 17
Souris Lake, 109
Souris River, 109
Speke, John Hanning, 128, 130
Speke Gulf, 130
spits, 51, 136
Stanley, Henry Morton, 129
St. Lawrence River, 15, 97, 104
St. Lawrence Seaway, 100, 102, 103
St. Louis River, 97, 105
St. Marys River, 99, 100, 105, 107, 172
Stokhid River, 174
stratification, 5, 36
streamflow, 54–55, 82
Sturgeon River, 106
Styr River, 174
Sulak River, 88

Sumatra, 12
Sundarbans, 152, 175
Superior, Lake, 1, 24, 61, 97, 98, 103, 105–109, 129
surface waters, 43, 57, 59, 65, 68
surface waves, 42, 46–48
Suwanee River, 172
swamps, 132, 133–134, 144, 147, 149, 153, 157–162, 164, 165, 173
Syr Darya, 3

T

Tahoe, Lake, 10
Tahquamenon River, 106
Tanganyika, Lake, 1, 11, 61, 127–129
Taquari River, 146
tectonism, 8, 10, 12
temperature patterns, 4–5
temporary waters, 1, 65–66, 70–71, 72
Terek River, 88
terrestrial ecosystems, 75, 132, 135, 151, 152
terrestrial primary production, 79
thermal gradients, 32, 35
thermal patterns, 68, 69
thermal plumes, 4
thermal pollution, 4, 37, 39
thermal stratification, 49, 70, 71

thermoclines, 32, 35, 45, 49
thin-shelf deposits, 8
tidal currents, 132
Tigris River, 170
Toba, Lake, 12
topography, basin, 17–19
transpiration, 121, 122
transverse seiching, 49
Treatise on Limnology, A, 8
Treig, Loch, 49
Trent River, 104
trophic levels, 75
trophogenic zone, 75–76
tropholytic zone, 76
tropical swamps, 158
Trummen, Lake, 23
Tuborg, Lake, 34
Tüpqaraghan, 88
turnovers, 26, 31

U

Uda River, 113
Ukerewe Island, 130
UNESCO World Heritage
    sites, 175
Ungava Lake, 17
Upper Angara River, 113
Ural River, 88
Utah, 8, 10, 24, 109, 110

V

varved deposits, 21
vertical gradients, 42, 57

vertical mixing, 30–31
Vetter, Lake, 49
Victoria, Lake, 55, 61, 129–131
volcanism, 8, 11–12, 66
Volga River, 87, 88, 93

W

Washington, George, 168
waste heat, 36–37
water balance, 6, 52–53,
    64–65, 116
water budget, 52, 53–59
water density, 30–31
waterfalls, 16
water input, 54–56, 71
water-level fluctuations,
    59–61
water levels, 42, 53, 59–61
water output, 56–59, 71
water quality, 7
water volume declines,
    40–41
wave height, 46–48
waves, 19, 20, 21, 44,
    45–48, 50–52, 94, 132–
    133, 138
Weber River, 109, 112
Welland Canal, 104
Western Rift Valley, 127, 129
wetlands, 150–152,
    162–176
White River, 101, 106
wildlife refuges, 168, 172, 178

Wiler, Lake, 23
wind-driven currents, 132
winds, 6, 8, 17, 20, 32, 34, 35,
    42, 44–45, 46, 47, 48,
    49, 57, 68, 91, 92, 94,
    126, 132
Winnipeg, Lake, 80, 109, 131
Winnipeg River, 131
Wisconsin, 14–15, 32
Wizard Island, 12

X

Xau, Lake, 171

Y

Yedseram River, 122
Yugoslavia, 16
Yukon River, 17

Z

Zambezi River, 126, 172
Zhilinsky, I.I., 174
Zoigê Marsh, 175–176
zonation, 141–142
zone of aeration, 56
zooplankton, 76–77
Zürich, Lake, 6